Collins · *do brilliantly !*

EightWeeks**Flat**

KS3 Maths

Helen Greaves

INTRODUCTION

Does this sound like you?

You know you should have started earlier but you haven't. The National Tests are just a few weeks away and you haven't even thought about revising because you thought you had ages. Or is it because you hate the whole revision thing – hours of staring at dull text books and badly taken class notes? Well don't despair, help is at hand in the form of *Eight Weeks Flat KS3 Maths*.

Why Eight Weeks Flat?

This colourful, easy-to-follow revision guide will help you prepare for those important Tests. The book covers material at levels 4, 5 and 6 and is mainly designed for students hoping to gain a level 5 or 6 in Maths at Key Stage 3.

Eight Weeks Flat KS3 Maths follows a week-by-week, day-by-day plan to help you break down your revision into small chunks. The plan is designed to spread your revision out into 40 sessions to be completed over eight weeks. However, if you started a bit earlier, follow the plan but you can give yourself an occasional day off or use the time to redo a topic you are not so sure about. If you have cut it a bit fine by leaving yourself less than eight weeks, aim to cover two topics each evening or do some at the weekends too.

How Eight Weeks Flat works

Each weekday you tackle a different topic. Each revision session consists of a page of important subject content and a page of follow-up practice activities.

Start by reading the notes, important facts, tips and examples on the topic. Try to learn any formulas or facts you need to remember. This should take you a few minutes. Words in **bold** appear in the Glossary on page 91. If you are not sure of the meaning of any of them, look them up!

When you think you are ready, turn over the page and try to answer all the questions about the topic you have just studied. The questions include some easy ones as well as some more difficult ones. Try them all – you don't get any marks for questions you miss out. You may wish to set yourself a time to complete the questions. This may help you to focus on attempting the questions rather than staring at the wall. Why not promise yourself a treat when you've finished?

Detailed answers and advice on how to mark the questions are provided at the back of the book (see page 92). Mark them yourself or get someone at home to do it for you. Add up your score and see how you have done. Use the 'How did you score?' box at the bottom of each question page to help judge your performance.

After you have completed all 40 revision sessions have a go at the Practice test (see page 85). This test includes questions on most topics. It starts with the easier questions and gets more difficult towards the end. Allow yourself an hour to complete it. Only use a calculator where allowed – no cheating!

Ask someone to mark your Practice test or do it yourself. Add up your marks and use the Level table at the end of the mark scheme (see page 96) to help decide the level you achieved. Remember – this is just an indication of your actual level.

If you have worked your way through the book and still have some time left for revision, go back and have another go at some of the sessions you didn't do so well the first time.

Best of luck!

About the National Tests

Just in case you are not sure how it all works, here is some information about the actual Tests.

At the beginning of May in Year 9 you will sit National Tests in Mathematics (as well as in English and Science). The Maths Tests are available in four tiers – levels 3–5, levels 4–6, levels 5–7 and levels 6–8. Your teacher will decide which tier to enter you for. Each KS3 Maths Test will include questions on number, algebra, shape, space, measures and handling data and will also test your ability to use and apply maths. You will take three Tests altogether:

Paper 1	60 marks	1 hour	calculator **not** allowed
Paper 2	60 marks	1 hour	calculator allowed
Mental test	30 marks	about 30 mins	calculator **not** allowed

In each Test the questions get harder as you work through them. Make sure you have the correct equipment with you for each Test. You are expected to have a pen, pencil, ruler, eraser, protractor and compasses, and a calculator for Paper 2 (preferably one which you are familiar with and know how to use!).

The completed Tests are sent away to be marked. You should find out how you have done in July. Most Year 9 pupils get a level 5 or 6 in the Maths National Tests.

CONTENTS

REVISION CHECKLIST

	Page numbers	Revised?
Number		
Place value and powers of 10	5–6	
Negative numbers	7–8	
Multiples, factors, primes and squares	19–20	
Rounding and estimation	35–36	
Fractions	45–46	
Fractions, decimals, percentages	47–48	
Calculations with fractions	55–56	
Using fractions and percentages	65–66	
Ratio and proportion	67–68	
Calculations		
The four number operations	15–16	
Powers, roots and order of operations	17–18	
Using a calculator	37–38	
Algebra		
Algebraic terms and expressions	9–10	
Rules and formulas	27–28	
Sequences	39–40	
Functions and mappings	49–50	
Straight line graphs	57–58	
Equations	69–70	
Shape, space and measures		
Metric and imperial units	11–12	
2D shapes	13–14	
Perimeter and area	21–22	
Area formulas	29–30	
Measuring and constructions	31–32	
Circles	41–42	
3D shapes	51–52	
Time	59–60	
Volume and surface area of cuboids	61–62	
Angles	71–72	
Symmetry, reflections and rotations	75–76	
Translation and enlargement	77–78	
Handling data		
Probability	23–24	
Collecting data	33–34	
Mode, median, mean and range	43–44	
Charts for displaying data	53–54	
Scatter diagrams	63–64	
Pie charts	73–74	
Using and applying maths to solve problems		
Solving problems	25–26	
Using number and algebra facts	79–80	
Using shape and space facts	81–82	
Using data and probability	83–84	

PLACE VALUE AND POWERS OF 10

What you need to know

1 Compare and order both whole and decimal numbers.

2 Multiply and divide both whole and decimal numbers by 10, 100, 1000.

PLACE VALUE

- The position of a digit in a number determines its value. Each position has a value of ten times more than the one to its right and ten times less than the one to its left.

Examples   Look at the number 13 842 690:

tens of millions	millions	hundreds of thousands	tens of thousands	thousands	hundreds	tens	units
1	3	8	4	2	6	9	0

In this whole number, or **integer**, the digit 6 has a value of 6 hundreds, 600.
The digit 4 has a value of 4 ten thousands, 40 000.

Look at the number 1.6724:

units	tenths	hundredths	thousandths	ten thousandths
1	6	7	2	4

In this decimal number the digit 6 has a value of 6 tenths, 0.6.
The digit 4 has a value of 4 ten thousandths, 0.0004.

Remember
> means greater than
< means less than

Quick Tip
Compare numbers by comparing the digits with the same place value.
0.378 is smaller than 0.38 because the *hundredths* digit in 0.378 is 7 compared to a *hundredths* digit of 8 in 0.38.

MULTIPLYING BY 10, 100, 1000

- Each digit moves to the left.

Examples

43 x 10 =	4 3 0	0.062 x 10 =	0 . 6 2
43 x 100 =	4 3 0 0	0.062 x 100 =	6 . 2
43 x 1000 =	4 3 0 0 0	0.062 x 1000 = 6 2	

DIVIDING BY 10, 100, 1000

- Each digit moves to the right.

Examples

79000 ÷ 10 =	7 9 0 0	25 ÷ 10 =	2 . 5
79000 ÷ 100 =	7 9 0	25 ÷ 100 =	0 . 2 5
79000 ÷ 1000 =	7 9	25 ÷ 1000 =	0 . 0 2 5

PLACE VALUE AND POWERS OF 10

1 Here are four number cards.

A	**B**	**C**	**D**
43020	forty thousand, three hundred and twenty	forty three thousand and two	40302

403 40320   *43,002*

Arrange them in order of size starting with the smallest. *40302, 43020, 43,002, 40320*   1 mark

2 Here is a number statement.
Is the statement **true**? Tick (✓) Yes or No.

$$4.86 > 4.9$$

Yes ☐   No ☒   Explain how you know. *If you put* ~~~~   1 mark

3 Look at these numbers.

7.32	0.723	37.2	732	0.732

(a) Which is the smallest number? *0.723*   1 mark

(b) Which number has 2 as its **tenths** digit? *37.2*   1 mark

(c) Which two numbers have the same **hundredths** digit? *7.32, 0.723*   1 mark

4 Here are some number cards.

43	430	0.43	0.0043	4300

(a) Which number is 100 times bigger than 4.3? *430*   1 mark

(b) Which number is 100 times smaller than 43?   1 mark

5 Here are four digit cards.

1	9	6	5

(a) Arrange the digits to give the number that is closest to 6000. *5 961*   1 mark

(b) Arrange the digits to give the number that is closest to 5500. *5619*   1 mark

6 Write numbers in the boxes to complete each calculation.

(a) 0.7 × *100* = 700   (b) *0.22* × 10 = 2.2   2 marks

(c) 7.8 ÷ *10* = 0.78   (d) *400* ÷ 1000 = 0.04   2 marks

7 Mrs Reed orders these items for the maths department. **Without using a calculator** work out the total cost of the order.

> 100 protractors at 23p each
> 1000 exercise books at 45p each
> 10 calculators at £6.49 each

3 marks

£23.00
£450.00 → *473.00*
£64.9 — 64.4 → *£537.9*

TOTAL ☐

NEGATIVE NUMBERS

What you need to know

1 Compare and order negative numbers.

2 Perform simple calculations involving negative numbers.

NUMBER LINE

- On a number line, the further a number is to the **left**, the **smaller** it is. The further the number to the **right**, the **larger** it is.

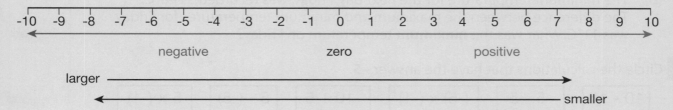

Remember

Negative numbers may be written in different ways.

−3   (−3)   ⁻3

all mean the same thing.

SIMPLE + AND − CALCULATIONS

- To work out the answer to **2 − 5**, start at 2 and count **back** 5 (1, 0, −1, −2, −3) down to −3. So 2 − 5 = −3.
- To work out the answer to **−7 + 6**, start at −7 and count **on** 6 (−6, −5, −4, −3, −2, −1) up to −1.   So −7 + 6 = −1.
- You can do this mentally or use a number line if you get stuck.

HARDER + AND − CALCULATIONS

- **Adding** a negative number results in **subtraction**.

Examples   2 + (−3) = 2 − 3 = −1   (−2) + (−3) = −2 − 3 = −5

- **Subtracting** a negative number results in **addition**.

Examples   2 − (−3) = 2 + 3 = 5   (−2) − (−3) = −2 + 3 = 1

MULTIPLYING AND DIVIDING

- The same rule is true for multiplying and dividing negative numbers.
- If **one** of the numbers is negative the answer will be **negative**.

Examples   2 x (−3) = −6   8 ÷ (−4) = −2
                (−2) x 3 = −6   (−8) ÷ 4 = −2

- If **both** of the numbers are negative the answer will be **positive**.

Examples   (−2) x (−3) = 6   (−8) ÷ (−4) = 2

Quick Tip

Negative numbers are used in everyday life. Examples include temperatures, money, scores in games. The rules are the same in these situations.

NEGATIVE NUMBERS

1 Holly has recorded the maximum and minimum temperatures for four days in January. Her results are shown in the table.

Day	Maximum temperature (°C)	Minimum temperature (°C)
Monday	3	–7
Tuesday	6	–5
Wednesday	–1	–10
Thursday	0	–8

(a) On which day was the **difference** between the maximum and minimum temperatures the greatest? *Wednesday*

1 mark

(b) The minimum temperature for the next day, Friday, was recorded as –8°C. The difference between the maximum and minimum temperatures for Friday was 11°C. What was the **maximum** temperature on Friday? *3°C*

1 mark

2 Circle the calculations that have the answer **–5**.

 10 - 15   -5 - 5   (-5) x (-1)   -10 + 5   5 - (-5)   5 x (-1)

2 marks

3 In a quiz, points are awarded using these rules:
  Score **3** points for a **correct** answer
  Score **–2** points for an **incorrect** answer.

(a) Kelly answers 4 questions correctly and 5 incorrectly. What is her total score?

1 mark

(b) Liam answers 3 questions correctly and 6 incorrectly. What is his total score?

1 mark

4 Put <, > or = into each statement to make it correct.

(a) (–2) – 5 ___>___ 3 – (–4)   (b) 3 – 9 ___<___ 8 ÷ (–2)

2 marks

5 Alice, Sandeep and Ashraf are playing a board game. The number of squares each player must move is worked out by finding the **product** of the scores on these two spinners.

If the product of the scores is **positive** then the player moves **forward** that number of squares. If the product is **negative** then the player must move that number of squares **backwards**.

(a) Alice scores –3 and –2 on the spinners. What move does she make? *5 Backwards*

1 mark

(b) Sandeep scores 3 and –1 on the spinners. What move does she make? *2 Forward*

1 mark

(c) To win, Ashraf needs to move forward exactly two squares. Give the **two** possible pairs of scores he needs to achieve this.

1 mark

6 Here are some number cards.   -7 -3 -2 -1 1 2 6

Choose two cards to complete each calculation.

(a) ☐ + ☐ = –8   (b) ☐ – ☐ = 9

(c) ☐ + ☐ = –2   *3 marks*

TOTAL ☐

ALGEBRAIC TERMS AND EXPRESSIONS

What you need to know

1 Use letters to represent unknown numbers in **terms** and **expressions**.

2 Simplify algebraic expressions by collecting like terms and multiplying out brackets.

USING LETTERS

- Letters can be used to represent unknown numbers.

Example Let a number be represented by the letter a.

In words	Algebraic term or expression
add 7 to the number	$a + 7$
multiply the number by 6	$6a$
add 2 to the number and multiply the result by 5	$5(a + 2)$
divide the number by 3 then add 1	$\dfrac{a}{3} + 1$
multiply the number by itself	a^2

ADDING AND SUBTRACTING TERMS

- Like **terms**, that is terms with the same letter or combination of letters, can be added and subtracted just like numbers.

Examples
$2b + b + 5b = 8b$ $7a + 3 - 6a + 2 = a + 5$

$2a + 3a + 3b + b = 5a + 4b$ $2pq + 5qr + 4qp = 6pq + 5qr$

$3n + 2n^2 + n + n^2 = 4n + 3n^2$

> **Remember**
> 'a multiplied by 3' is written as $3a$ rather than $3 \times a$ or $a3$.
> 'a divided by 5' is written as $\frac{a}{5}$ rather than $a \div 5$.
> 'a multiplied by itself' is written as a^2 rather than $a \times a$ or aa.

MULTIPLYING TERMS

- Multiply the numbers in the terms together and multiply the letters together.

Examples $2 \times 5b = 10b$ $2c \times 2d = 4cd$ $d \times d = d^2$ $(-2) \times 3m = -6m$

- For brackets, multiply the terms inside the bracket by the number or term outside the bracket.

Examples $2(4 + 3a) = 2 \times 4 + 2 \times 3a = 8 + 6a$

$p(p - 7) = p \times p - p \times 7 = p^2 - 7p$

> **Remember**
> pq and qp **are** like terms but n and n^2 are **not** like terms.
> The rules for adding and subtracting negative numbers apply to negative algebraic terms too.
> $2y + (-7y) = 2y - 7y = -5y$
> $3m - (-2m) = 3m + 2m = 5m$

ALGEBRAIC TERMS AND EXPRESSIONS

1 Ian is thinking of a number. He calls his number **n**.

(a) Write an expression for **his number multiplied by 5**.   1 mark

$5n$

(b) Write an expression for **his number added to 5 then double the resul**t.   1 mark

$10n$

2 Paul is **j** years old and Jack is **k** years old.
Jack is older than Paul.

(a) Write an expression for how much older Jack is than Paul.   1 mark

(b) Write an expression for Jack's age in 3 years' time.   1 mark

(c) Sally is twice as old as Paul. Write an expression for Sally's age.   1 mark

3 Write each expression in its simplest form.

(a) $m + 3 + m + 1$ (b) $9h + 2h - 5h$

(c) $4b + 9 + 2b + 8$ (d) $2a + 7m + 3a - 3m$

(e) $6st - 3ts + 4st$ (f) $6p + 3p + p^2 + 3p^2$ 6 marks

4 Kim has two bags of £1 coins.

 $n + 3$  $2n$

(a) Write a **simplified** expression for the total number of coins.   1 mark

(b) Kim takes all the coins and divides them into three equal piles.
Circle the expression that represents the number of coins in each pile.

$3n + 3$ $3n$ $n + 1$ $n - 1$ n $3n - 1$ 1 mark

5 Simplify each expression.

(a) $4a + (-2a)$ (b) $7m - (-m)$

(c) $5(3a + 1)$ (d) $n(n + 2)$

(e) $3(m + 2) + 2(m + 1)$ 5 marks

TOTAL ☐

METRIC AND IMPERIAL UNITS

What you need to know

1 Know the relationships between metric units of length, mass and capacity.

2 Convert between quantities measured in metric units.

3 Know and use the approximate metric equivalents of imperial units still in everyday use.

METRIC UNITS

Length	Mass	Capacity
1 cm = 10 mm	1 g = 1000 mg	1 ml = 1 cm³
1 m = 100 cm	1 kg = 1000 g	1 cl = 10 ml
1 m = 1000 mm	1 tonne = 1000 kg	1 l = 100 cl
1 km = 1000 m		1 l = 1000 ml

Quick Tip
In a question including units, always convert all quantities to the same units before doing any calculations.

CONVERTING BETWEEN METRIC UNITS

- To convert from a 'large' unit to a 'small' unit **multiply** by the conversion factor.

Example   3.6 kg = 3.6 x 1000 = 3600 g | 1 kg = 1000 g |

- To convert from a 'small' unit to a 'large' unit **divide** by the conversion factor.

Example   859 cm = 859 ÷ 100 = 8.59 m | 1 m = 100 cm |

IMPERIAL UNITS

Length

1 inch ≈ 2.5 cm   1 foot ≈ 30 cm   1 mile ≈ 1.6 km
                     1 foot = 12 inches   5 miles ≈ 8 km

Mass

1 ounce ≈ 30 g   1 pound ≈ 450 g   2.2 pounds ≈ 1 kg
                     1 pound = 16 ounces

Capacity

1 pint ≈ 0.5 litres 1 gallon ≈ 4.5 litres
                     1 gallon = 8 pints

Remember
≈ means is approximately equal to.

Examples   Convert 30 miles to km.
Either   30 x 1.6 = 48 km   or   since   5 miles = 8 km
                                      then   6 x 5 miles   = 6 x 8 km
                                                            = 48 km

A car petrol tank holds 36 litres. How many gallons is this?
36 ÷ 4.5 = 8 gallons

METRIC AND IMPERIAL UNITS

1 Convert these metric measures.

(a) 8 m = _____ cm

(b) 9000 g = _____ kg

(c) 23 l = _____ ml

(d) 5 ml = _____ cm³

(e) 350 cm = _____ m

(f) 4.5 kg = _____ g

(g) 5.2 l = _____ cl

(h) 0.7 g = _____ mg

(i) 450 m = _____ km

(j) 5800 mm = _____ m

10 marks

2 Circle the heaviest of these masses.

0.03 kg   300 g   3000 mg   30 g

1 mark

3 Oliver walks 1.2 km then jogs 700 m to get to the post office.
How far away is the post office? Give your answer in km.

1 mark

4 A shopkeeper measures out 4 kg of peanuts into bags each containing 250 g.
How many of these bags can he fill?

1 mark

5 Harry has a 1.5 litre bottle of cola. He drinks 850 ml of the cola.
How much cola is left in the bottle? Give your answer in litres.

1 mark

6 Complete these statements.

(a) 6 ounces is approximately _____ grams.

(b) 15 miles is approximately _____ km.

(c) 3 kg is equivalent to about _____ pounds.

(d) There are about 18 litres in _____ gallons.

4 marks

TOTAL [   ]

2D SHAPES

What you need to know

1 Know and use the properties of triangles, **quadrilaterals** and **polygons**.

TRIANGLES

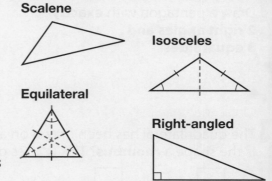

- Angles add up to 180°.
- Scalene triangle – no equal sides or angles.
- Isosceles triangle – two equal sides and angles, one line of symmetry.
- Equilateral triangle – all sides equal, all angles 60°, 3 lines of symmetry.
- Right-angled triangle – one 90° angle (can be isosceles if other two angles are each 45°).

QUADRILATERALS

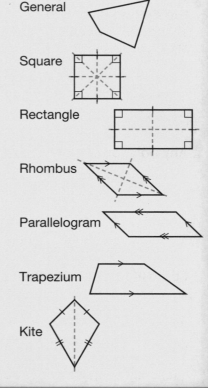

- Angles add up to 360°.
- General **quadrilateral** – no equal sides or angles (one angle can be bigger than 180°).
- Square – all sides equal, all angles 90°, opposite sides **parallel**, **diagonals** are equal and **bisect** at right angles, 4 lines of symmetry.
- Rectangle – two pairs of equal sides, all angles 90°, opposite sides parallel, diagonals are equal and bisect each other, 2 lines of symmetry.
- Rhombus – all sides equal, opposite angles equal, opposite sides parallel, diagonals bisect at right angles, 2 lines of symmetry.
- Parallelogram – two pairs of equal sides, opposite angles equal, opposite sides parallel, diagonals bisect each other, no lines of symmetry.
- Trapezium – one pair of parallel sides, no lines of symmetry.
- Kite – two pairs of **adjacent** sides are equal, one pair of equal opposite angles, diagonals cross at right angles, one line of symmetry.

POLYGONS

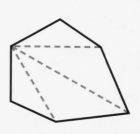

- A **polygon** has straight sides:
  a pentagon has 5 sides, a hexagon has 6, a heptagon 7, an octagon 8, a nonagon 9, a decagon 10.
- A **regular** polygon has all sides equal and all angles equal.
- A polygon can be divided into triangles to work out the sum of its angles. For example, a hexagon can be divided into 4 triangles so its angles add up to 720° (= 4 x 180°).

2D SHAPES

1 The triangle has been drawn on a square grid.
Which **two** types of triangle is it?

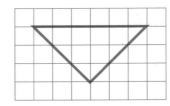

1 mark

2 Draw a pentagon with **exactly**
2 right angles and
3 equal sides.

1 mark

3 The quadrilateral has been drawn on a square grid.
Is the shape a **rhombus**? Tick (✓) Yes or No.

Yes ☐   No ☐   Explain how you know.

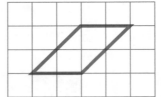

1 mark

4 On the dotty square grids
the **diagonals** of two
shapes have been drawn.
Name each shape.

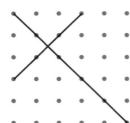
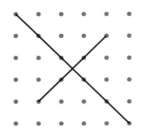

2 marks

5 Any polygon can be divided into triangles as shown below:

quadrilateral   hexagon
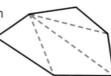

(a) The sum of the angles inside a quadrilateral is 360°.
     Explain how you know.

1 mark

(b) What is the sum of the angles inside a **hexagon**?

1 mark

(c) One type of polygon has inside angles that add up to 1080°.
     How many **sides** does it have?

1 mark

6 Work out the size of the angles marked *a* and *b*.

a = _____

b = _____

2 marks

TOTAL ☐

How did you score?

4 or less – try again!
5 – 7 – nearly there!
8 – 10 – well done!

THE FOUR NUMBER OPERATIONS

What you need to know

1 Use the four number operations of addition, subtraction, multiplication and division on whole and decimal numbers.

CALCULATIONS

- Being able to add, subtract, multiply and divide numbers are essential skills. Make sure you can accurately carry out a variety of number calculations without using a calculator.
- Always line up digits neatly in the correct columns to avoid mistakes.

Examples $3079 - 978$ $38.5 + 9.67 + 8$

$$^2\!3^1079$$
$$978 -$$
$$2101$$

$$38.50$$
$$9.67 +$$
$$8.00$$
$$56.17$$

put 0's in the gaps if it helps

- Know your multiplication tables inside out – they are essential for both multiplication *and* division.

Example $545 \div 8$

need to know
7 x 8 = 56 too big!
6 x 8 = 48

$$8)5^54^65 \quad 0\,6\,8\ r1$$

need to know
8 x 8 = 64

- There are a number of methods for 'long' multiplication and division. Make sure you know and can use a method that works for you. Here are a couple of methods which many people find useful.

Examples 39×28

x	30	9
20	600	180
8	240 +	72 +
	840	252

840
252 +
1092

$39 \times 28 = 1092$

$374 \div 17$

$$374$$
10 x 17 $170-$
$$204$$
10 x 17 $170-$
$$34$$
2 x 17 $34-$
22   0

10 x 17 = 170
5 x 17 = 85
2 x 17 = 34

$374 \div 17 = 22$

- Don't forget these techniques for multiplying and dividing two decimal numbers.

Examples 0.4×0.7 do 4 x 7 to get 28 then 'add' 2 decimal places to get 0 . 2 8
0.6×0.03 do 6 x 3 to get 18 then 'add' 3 decimal places to get 0 . 0 1 8
$0.6 \div 0.2$ multiply **both** numbers by 10 to get 6 ÷ 2 = 3
$0.8 \div 0.04$ multiply **both** numbers by 100 to get 80 ÷ 4 = 20

THE FOUR NUMBER OPERATIONS

Do not use a calculator for any of these questions.

1 Calculate:

(a) 464 – 289   (b) 138 x 9   *2 marks*

(c) 861 ÷ 7   (d) 1398 + 4067   *2 marks*

2 Work out:

(a) 13.6 + 8 + 4.82   (b) 49.3 – 23.68   *2 marks*

(c) 4.78 x 6   (d) 32.24 ÷ 8   *2 marks*

3 Evaluate:

(a) 0.3 x 0.4   *1 mark*

(b) 0.5 x 0.07   *1 mark*

(c) 0.05 x 0.09   *1 mark*

4 Evaluate:

(a) 0.8 ÷ 0.2   *1 mark*

(b) 0.35 ÷ 0.05   *1 mark*

5 Calculate 43 x 26.   *2 marks*

6 Calculate 336 ÷ 21.   *2 marks*

TOTAL

How did you score?

7 or less – try again!
8 – 13 – nearly there!
14 – 17 – well done!

POWERS, ROOTS AND ORDER OF OPERATIONS

What you need to know

1 Find **powers** and **roots** of some numbers.

2 Know the order in which to carry out operations in a calculation.

POWERS AND ROOTS

- A **power** has a base number and an index (the little number at the top). The index tells you how many of the number you multiply together.

5^3 means 5 x 5 x 5 = 125   It does not mean 5 x 3!

3^2 (said as 'three squared') = 3 x 3 = 9

4^3 (said as 'four cubed') = 4 x 4 x 4 = 64

2^4 (said as 'two to the power of four') = 2 x 2 x 2 x 2 = 16

- Finding the **root** of a number is the inverse operation to finding a power.

$\sqrt{9}$ (said as 'the square root of nine') means 'what number must be squared to give 9?'. The answer is 3.

$^3\sqrt{64}$ (said as 'the cube root of 64') means 'what number must be cubed to give 64?'. The answer is 4.

ORDER OF OPERATIONS

- The word BODMAS is used to remember the order in which to carry out operations in a calculation. You need to remember what the letters stand for –
  Brackets, p**O**wers, **D**ivide, **M**ultiply, **A**dd, **S**ubtract.

2 + 5 x 3 = 21 ✗   This is incorrect as the addition has been done before the multiplication.

2 + 5 x 3 = 17 ✓   This is correct as the multiplication has been done first.

Examples	$2^3 - 8 \div 2$	$= 8 - 8 \div 2$	$= 8 - 4$	$= 4$
		first do power	then divide	finally subtract
	$15 + (1 + 2)^2$	$= 15 + (3)^2$	$= 15 + 9$	$= 24$
		first do bracket	then power	finally add

17

POWERS, ROOTS AND ORDER OF OPERATIONS

1 Find the value of:

(a) 2^3

(b) 5^2

(c) 7^2

(d) 3^4

(e) 10^5

(f) 3^3

2 Find these square and cube roots.

(a) $\sqrt{81}$

(b) $\sqrt{64}$

(c) $\sqrt[3]{8}$

(d) $\sqrt[3]{1000}$

(e) $\sqrt{144}$

(f) $\sqrt[3]{125}$

3 Look at these numbers.

2^5 4^2 3^3 9^1 1^{10}

(a) Which is the largest number?

(b) Which number has the same value as $\sqrt{81}$?

4 Calculate:

(a) $14 - 2 \times 5$

(b) $23 - (2 + 8)$

(c) 3×2^2

(d) $5 + 3 \times 8 - 4$

(e) $20 \div 5 + 2^3$

(f) $(5 - 3)^2 + 6$

5 Put brackets into each calculation so that it has the answer shown.

(a) $6 + 3 \times 5 - 2 = 43$

(b) $6 + 3 \times 5 - 2 = 27$

TOTAL

MULTIPLES, FACTORS, PRIMES AND SQUARES

What you need to know

1. Find **factors** and **multiples** of a given number.
2. Find common factors and multiples of two or more numbers.
3. Recognise **square** and **prime numbers**.
4. Express a number as a **product** of prime factors.

COMMON FACTORS AND MULTIPLES

- Some numbers have common factors and all numbers have common multiples.

Examples   Factors of 18   1, 2, 3, **6**, **9**, 18
Factors of 30   1, 2, 3, 5, **6**, 10, 15, 30
18 and 30 have four common factors, the highest is 6.

Multiples of 4   **4**, **8**, **12**, **16**, 20, **24**, **28**, **32**, **36**, **40**, **44**, ...
Multiples of 5   **5**, **10**, **15**, 20, **25**, **30**, **35**, **40**, **45**, **50**, ...
4 and 5 have common multiples of 20, 40, 60, 80, ...
The lowest common multiple is 20.

> **Remember**
> Don't mix up **factors** and **multiples**. Multiples must be equal to or more than the number. For example, multiples of 7 are 7, 14, 21, 28, ...
> Think multiplication tables!

PRIME NUMBERS

- A **prime number** has only two factors, 1 and the number itself. 2 is the only even prime number. All other even numbers are non-prime because they all have 2 as a factor.
- 1 is not a prime number. The first few prime numbers are 2, 3, 5, 7, 11, 13, 17, 19, 23, 29, 31, ...
- Any non-prime number can be written as a **product** (multiplication) of prime numbers (factors).

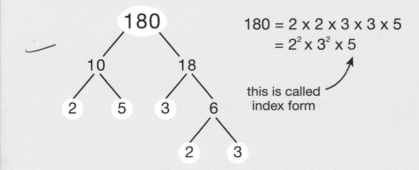

$180 = 2 \times 2 \times 3 \times 3 \times 5$
$= 2^2 \times 3^2 \times 5$

this is called index form

> **Quick Tip**
> One way to find factors of a number is to think of all the different pairs of numbers that multiply to give that number.
>
>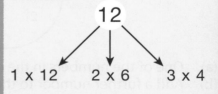
>
> factors of 12 are
> 1, 2, 3, 4, 6 and 12

SQUARE NUMBERS

- A **square number** is found by multiplying a number by itself, for example, 3 x 3 or $3^2 = 9$, 7 x 7 or $7^2 = 49$.
- A square number always has an odd number of factors.

MULTIPLES, FACTORS, PRIMES AND SQUARES

1 Circle all the prime numbers in the list of numbers below.

    17   1   9   22   5   39   8

1 mark

2 Write the number **126** as a product of prime factors (numbers).

2 marks

3 Andrea is 14 years old. Her brother Ben is 24 years old.
  (a)   Write down all of the **factors** of 14.

1 mark

  (b)   How old will Ben be when his age is next a **multiple** of **both** 2 and 7?

1 mark

  (c)   Last year Andrea and Ben's ages were both prime numbers.
       Andrea was 13 years old when Ben was 23 years old.
       How many years will it be before their ages are again **both** prime numbers?

1 mark

4 (a)   The number 9 can be written as two different pairs of factors.

> $9 = 1 \times 9$ $9 = 3 \times 3$
> The factors of 9 are 1, 3 and 9.

       Complete the following information for the number 16.

       16 = _____ x _____   16 = _____ x _____   16 = _____ x _____

       The factors of 16 are _____, _____, _____, _____ and _____ .

1 mark

  (b)   The numbers 9 and 16 are both square numbers. They both have an odd number of factors. Explain why all square numbers have an odd number of factors.

1 mark

5 Look at the diagram.

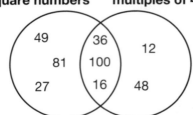

square numbers   multiples of 4

49   36   12   81   100   27   16   48

  (a)   One of the numbers in the diagram is incorrect. Put a cross through it.

1 mark

  (b)   Add a further number to the diagram that is **both** a square number and a multiple of 4.

1 mark

6 Paul has been asked to set out **48** desks for an exam.
He must arrange them in rows with the same number of desks in each row. There must not be more than 20 desks in each row and there must be no more than 10 rows.
List the **four** different arrangements that are possible.

2 marks

TOTAL [   ]

How did you score?

5 or less – try again!
6 – 8 – nearly there!
9 – 12 – well done!

PERIMETER AND AREA

What you need to know

1 Work out the **perimeter** of a 2D shape.

2 Find the **area** of some 2D shapes by counting squares.

PERIMETER

- The **perimeter** is the distance around the outside of a 2D shape. Its units are therefore length units, such as mm, cm, m, km, inches.

- It is easy to find the perimeter if the length of each side is known. For some shapes you may first need to work out the lengths of any unknown sides.

Example Here are two tiles. The tiles are put together to make a shape. Find the perimeter of the shape.

You first need to work out the unknown side.

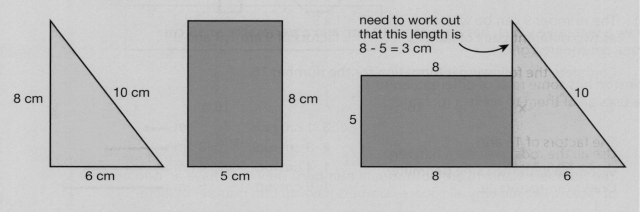

Perimeter = 10 + 6 + 8 + 5 + 8 + **3** = 40 cm

AREA

- The **area** is the amount of space inside a 2D shape. Its units are square units, such as mm², cm², m².

- If a shape is drawn on a grid it may be possible to work out its area by counting the number of squares.

Shapes A and B have the same area of 6 cm² (shape B has 5 whole and 2 half squares). Just because they have the same area does not mean they have the same perimeter. A has a perimeter of 10 cm (count ten 1 cm lengths around the edges). B has a larger perimeter as the two diagonal sides are longer than 1 cm (count eight 1 cm lengths and two > 1 cm lengths).

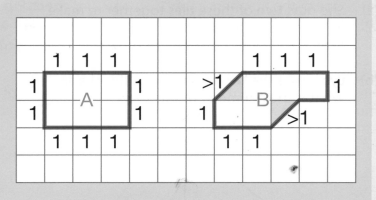

PERIMETER AND AREA

1 Look at the shape on the grid.
Each square has a side of 1 cm.

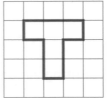

Not actual size

(a) Write down both the **perimeter** and **area** of the shape.

Perimeter = _____ cm   Area = _____ cm²

1 mark

(b) Draw a shape with an area of 6 cm² and a perimeter of 12 cm.

1 mark

2 Look at the shapes on the grid.
Four of the five shapes have the same area.
Which shape has a different area to the other four?

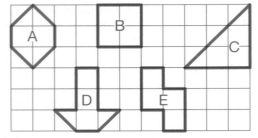

1 mark

3 Draw a rectangle which has an **area of 12 cm²** and a **perimeter of 16 cm**.
Use a cm squared grid.

1 mark

4 Winston has some rods of different lengths.
He uses all of them to make a rectangle.

3 1 cm rods   1 cm ┣━┫
2 3 cm rods   3 cm ┣━━━┫
1 4 cm rod   4 cm ┣━━━━┫
1 5 cm rod   5 cm ┣━━━━━┫

(a) Use all the rods to make a different rectangle with the same perimeter.
Draw your rectangle.

1 mark

(b) Is it possible to make a square using all of the rods?
Tick (✓) Yes or No.

Yes ☐   No ☐

Not actual size

Explain your answer.

1 mark

5 Lydia has some triangular tiles like the one shown.

not accurately drawn

(a) She puts **two** of these tiles together to make an **isosceles** triangle with a **perimeter of 16 cm**.
Sketch and label a diagram to show this isosceles triangle.

5 cm   3 cm

4 cm

1 mark

(b) Lydia uses the two tiles to make this shape.
What is the perimeter of this shape?

1 mark

not accurately drawn

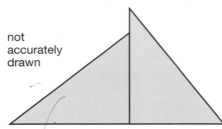

TOTAL ☐

PROBABILITY

What you need to know

1 Identify **outcomes** of an **event** and calculate their probabilities.

2 Know that probabilities lie between 0 and 1 and can be expressed as fractions, decimals or percentages.

SIMPLE PROBABILITY

- The probability of an **outcome** is the number of ways of getting that outcome divided by the total number of possible outcomes.

Example

Probability of picking a star = $\frac{2}{10}$ (number of stars in bag)

                        (total number of shapes in bag)

P (star) = $\frac{1}{5}$ (simplified fraction)

This probability can be shown on a probability scale.

 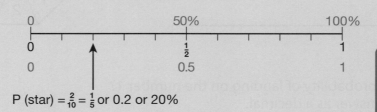

P (star) = $\frac{2}{10} = \frac{1}{5}$ or 0.2 or 20%

- Some **events** have equally likely outcomes. For example, tossing a coin has two outcomes, heads or tails, and each has a probability of $\frac{1}{2}$. However, some events do not have equally likely outcomes. For example, there are two outcomes when taking an exam, passing or failing. The probability of each is not necessarily $\frac{1}{2}$. It would depend on how difficult the exam is.

> **Remember**
> All probabilities have a value of between 0 and 1. Probabilities are written as fractions, decimals or percentages.

COMBINED EVENTS

- If two or more events are combined, you need to make sure you identify all the possible outcomes.

Examples

A vending machine dispenses tea or coffee that can be white or black. There are four possible outcomes – white tea, black tea, white coffee, black coffee.

A door lock uses a security code – a letter (A or B) followed by a number (7, 8 or 9). There are six possible outcomes. These can be shown in a diagram, sometimes called a possibility space.

	A	B
7	A 7	B 7
8	A 8	B 8
9	A 9	B 9

The number of outcomes could be increased by allowing a letter and number in any order. This would give 12 possible codes. The extra six would be 7A, 8A, 9A, 7B, 8B and 9B.

PROBABILITY

1 Zoe has 10 white counters and 10 black counters.
She puts a total of 10 counters into a bag.
How many of each colour should she put into the bag to give the following situations?

(a) There is an even chance of picking a white counter.

(b) The probability of picking a white counter is 0.

(c) There is a greater chance of picking a white counter than a black counter.

2 The diagram shows a spinner.

(a) Which number is the spinner most likely to land on?

(b) What is the probability of landing on the number 4?
Show your answer on the probability scale.

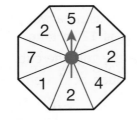

```
 |---|---|---|---|---|---|---|
 0                           1
```

(c) What is the probability of landing on the number 1?
Write your answer as a decimal.

3 As part of their school lunch, pupils can choose any **two** pieces of fruit from apples, pears, oranges and bananas.
List all the possible combinations that a pupil could choose.
(Use the letters **A**, **P**, **O**, **B** rather than writing out the full words.)

4 Here is a blank spinner divided into six equal sections.

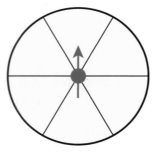

Write numbers on the spinner so that the probability of landing on an
odd number is $\frac{1}{3}$ and the probability of scoring a **5** is $\frac{1}{6}$.

5 Polly has a bag of mixed sweets. It contains some chocolates, some toffees and some mints.
Polly thinks that the probability of picking either a chocolate, toffee or mint is $\frac{1}{3}$.
Explain why this may not be true.

TOTAL [ ]

What you need to know

1 Choose and use the correct operation(s) to solve real-life problems.

TYPES OF PROBLEMS

- Many real-life maths problems can be solved using one or more of the four number operations. Simple problems may involve just one step – either an addition, subtraction, multiplication or division. However, you are more likely to have to solve problems with two or more steps in which you will need to use a combination of the four operations.

Examples

Nadia is using a wallpaper border to decorate a room. The roll of wallpaper border is **12 m** long.

From the roll she cuts **three** pieces **each 2.9 m** long and a piece **2.4 m** long. How much of the border roll is left over?

First work out the total length cut from the roll.

3 x 2.9 m =   8.7 m

2.4 m +

11.1 m

Then subtract this total length from 12 m.

12 – 11.1 = 0.9 m   so 0.9m is left over.

> This problem involves x, + and –.

Erin is buying a new computer for **£1560**. She pays **half** now and the rest in **four** equal payments over the next four months. How much is each of the monthly payments?

First work out half of the cost by dividing by 2.

£1560 ÷ 2 = £780

Then divide this amount by 4.

£780 ÷ 4 = £195   so the monthly payment is £195.

> This problem involves two divisions.

Remember

Work out how many steps are needed to solve the problem.
Identify the quantities or numbers to be used in each step – these are often in **bold** type in Test questions.
Decide which operation is needed for each step.
Carry out each step of the problem accurately using your calculation skills – **show all your working.**

SOLVING PROBLEMS

Do not use a calculator for any of these questions.

1 Ben buys a sandwich costing **£2.85**, a packet of crisps costing **47p** and a bottle of water for **£1**.
What is his change from a **£10** note?

2 marks

2 A shopkeeper bought a **2.5 kg** jar of jelly beans.
She sold **0.85 kg** of jelly beans on Monday and **500 g** of jelly beans on Tuesday.
What weight of jelly beans is left to sell on Wednesday?
Give your answer in kg.

2 marks

3 **1390** members of a football supporters club are planning to use coaches to travel to an away match. Each coach can carry **53** passengers.
How many coaches will be needed to carry all the supporters?

2 marks

4 An internet company sells DVDs and CDs. **Each DVD** costs **£11.50** and **each CD** costs **£6.75**. The company offers free delivery if the order is £50 or more. For orders under £50 a **£5** delivery charge is added to the total cost of the order.
Mr Reid orders **2 DVDs** and **4 CDs**.
Miss Quinn orders **3 DVDs** and **2 CDs**.
Work out the cost of each order remembering to add on a delivery charge if required.

2 marks

5 A school buys **18** boxes of crisps. Each box contains **48** packets of crisps.
(a) How many packets of crisps are there in 18 boxes?

2 marks

(b) The school sells them in the tuck shop and makes **5p** profit on each packet.
How much profit does the school make if it sells every packet?

1 mark

TOTAL

How did you score?
5 or less – try again!
6 – 8 – nearly there!
9 – 11 – well done!

RULES AND FORMULAS

What you need to know

1   Use rules in the form of words and flowcharts.

2   Substitute numbers in algebraic **formulas**.

RULES

* In maths, a rule can be written in words or shown in a flowchart.

Here is the rule for converting an amount in gallons to an amount in litres:

In words   Divide the amount in gallons by two then multiply by nine.

As a flowchart

amount in gallons   ⟶   ÷ 2   ⟶   x 9   ⟶ amount in litres

Using the rule to convert 6 gallons gives $6 \div 2 = 3$ then $3 \times 9 = 27$ litres.

FORMULAS

* More often in maths, rules are given as algebraic **formulas**. A formula uses letters and symbols. Different letters are used for different quantities.

* A formula can be used by substituting numbers for the letters.

Here is the rule for finding the perimeter of a square:

In words   The perimeter is four times the length of one side.

As a formula $P = 4a$ The letter P is used for perimeter.

                              The letter a is used for the length of a side.

> **Remember**
> In algebra $4a$ means $4 \times a$.

Using the formula to find the perimeter if $a = 7$ cm gives $P = 4 \times 7 = 28$ cm

Examples $P = 2m + n$ if $m = 5$ and $n = 3$ $P = 2 \times 5 + 3 = 10 + 3 = \mathbf{13}$

                  $A = q^2 - qr$ if $q = 7$ and $r = 2$ $A = 7^2 - 7 \times 2 = 49 - 14 = \mathbf{35}$

                  $M = \dfrac{a + b + c}{3}$ if $a = 5$, $b = 10$, $c = 3$ $M = \dfrac{5 + 10 + 3}{3} = \dfrac{18}{3} = \mathbf{6}$

In each case the letters are replaced by numbers and then the calculation is worked out.

> **Remember**
> Use the BODMAS rule here!

RULES AND FORMULAS

1 Here are rules to work out the times for roasting joints of meat.

      Beef   **20** minutes per pound plus an extra **15** minutes

      Pork   **25** minutes per pound plus an extra **25** minutes

(a) How many minutes are needed to roast a **2** pound joint of pork?

1 mark

(b) How many minutes are needed to roast a **3 $\frac{1}{2}$** pound joint of beef?

1 mark

2 A taxi driver uses this flowchart to work out the cost of a taxi fare.
The cost of the fare depends on the number of miles for the journey.

number of miles $\longrightarrow$ | **x 15 pence** | $\longrightarrow$ | **+ 65 pence** | $\longrightarrow$ | **÷ 100** | $\longrightarrow$ fare in £

(a) Use the flowchart to work out the fare for a 4 mile journey.

1 mark

(b) The taxi driver charges a passenger £2.15 for a journey.
How many miles was the journey?

1 mark

3 Here is a formula: $T = n - 5$.

(a) Work out the value of T when $n = 19$.

(b) Work out the value of T when $n = 3$.

2 marks

4 Here is a formula: $m = ab + c$.
Work out the value of m when $a = 5, b = 6$ and $c = 10$.

1 mark

5 Here is a formula: $q = \dfrac{x + y}{3z}$.

Work out the value of q when $x = 50, y = 10$ and $z = 2$.

1 mark

6 The formula for finding the perimeter of a rectangle is
$P = 2(l + w)$.
Use the formula to complete the table.

l	w	P
3	5	16
11	4	
2.5	4.5	
	6	18

3 marks

TOTAL ☐

How did you score?

5 or less – try again!
6 – 8 – nearly there!
9 – 11 – well done!

AREA FORMULAS

What you need to know

1 Use **formulas** to find the areas of rectangles, squares, triangles, parallelograms and trapeziums.

USING FORMULAS

- Some shapes have **formulas** that can be used to work out their areas.
  To use each formula you need to know certain **dimensions** of each shape.

- For a rectangle you need to know the length, l, and the width, w.
  For a square you need to know the length of a side, l.

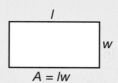
$A = lw$

$A = l^2$

> **Quick Tip**
> You need to learn these formulas. Apart from the trapezium formula they are not usually given to you in the Test papers.

- For a triangle, parallelogram and trapezium you need to know the **perpendicular** height, h, which is the distance from the base, of length b, to the top of the shape.

$A = \frac{1}{2} bh$

means $\frac{1}{2} \times b \times h$

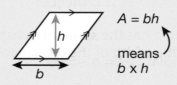
$A = bh$

means $b \times h$

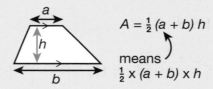
$A = \frac{1}{2} (a + b) h$

means $\frac{1}{2} \times (a + b) \times h$

Examples   Work out the area of the triangle.

$A = \frac{1}{2} \times 7 \times 8 = \frac{1}{2}$ of $56 = 28$ cm^2

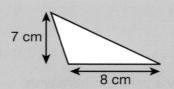
7 cm
8 cm

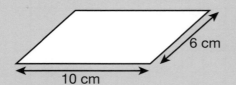
6 cm
10 cm

You cannot work out the area of the parallelogram as you don't know h.
h is not 6 cm.

Example   A rectangle has an area of 48 m^2. The length of the rectangle is 8 m.
What is the width of the rectangle?

$A = lw$

$48 = 8 \times w$

$w = 6$ m

AREA FORMULAS

1 For each shape use a suitable formula to work out its area. Write the correct units with each answer.

(a) 2.6 cm

10 cm

(b) 9 mm

(c)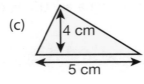
4 cm
5 cm

(d)
3 km 5 km
4 km

(e)
5 cm
8 cm

(f)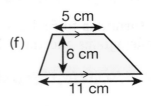
5 cm
6 cm
11 cm

(g)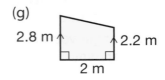
2.8 m 2.2 m
2 m

7 marks

2 (a) A square has an area of **64 cm²**. What is the length of each side?

1 mark

(b) A rectangle has the **same area** as the square and a length of **16 cm**. What is the width of the rectangle?

1 mark

3 (a) On the grid draw a triangle with an **area of 9 square units** and a **base of 6 units**.
Use the line AB as the base of your triangle.

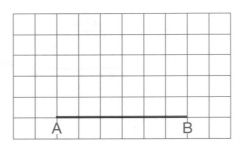

A   B

1 mark

(b) On the grid draw a parallelogram with an **area of 12 square units** and a **base of 6 units**.
Use the line AB as the base of your parallelogram.

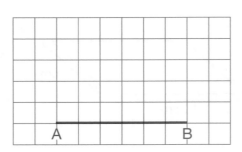

A   B

1 mark

TOTAL [   ]

How did you score?
5 or less – try again!
6 – 8 – nearly there!
9 – 11 – well done!

MEASURING AND CONSTRUCTIONS

What you need to know

1 Read scales on measuring equipment to the nearest division.

2 Measure straight lines to the nearest mm and angles to the nearest degree.

3 Construct diagrams using ruler, protractors and compasses.

READING SCALES

- To read a scale you need to work out what each division is worth.

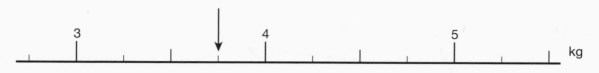

This scale has four divisions per kg so each division must be 0.25 kg.
The reading is therefore 3.75 kg.

MEASURING

- You should make sure you can draw and measure straight lines accurately.

- Using a protractor needs care. A protractor has two scales so that you can read it in two directions. Make sure you line up the protractor accurately, then read off the correct scale. Always measure round from 0°.

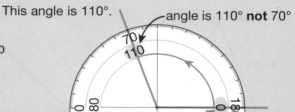

This angle is 110°.

angle is 110° **not** 70°

read off this scale

CONSTRUCTIONS

- You can construct a triangle if you know the sizes of some sides and/or angles.

- If you know the lengths of all 3 sides you can construct the triangle using a ruler and compasses only.

Draw one side using your ruler. Now set the compasses to the length of one of the other sides and draw an arc from one end of your first side. Do the same for the third side from the other end of your first side. Complete the triangle as shown.

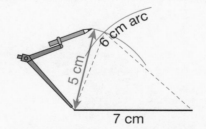

- If you know any angles you can use a protractor to construct them.

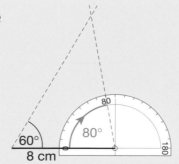

MEASURING AND CONSTRUCTIONS

1 Write down the reading shown by the arrow on each of these scales.

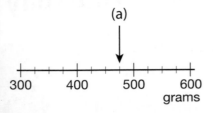 (a)

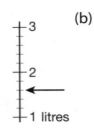 (b)

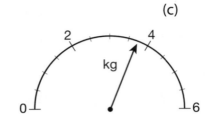 (c)

2 Measure these angles to the nearest degree.

(a)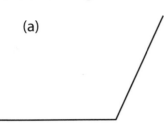

(b)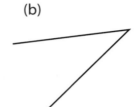

3 Construct an accurate drawing for each of the diagrams below.

(a)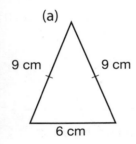

(b)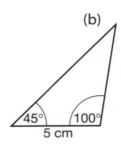

(c)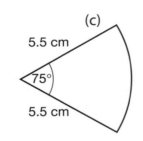

not accurately drawn

4 Look at the quadrilateral ABCD.

Complete an accurate drawing of the quadrilateral. Two sides have already been drawn for you.

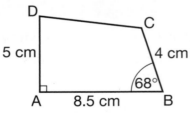

not accurately drawn

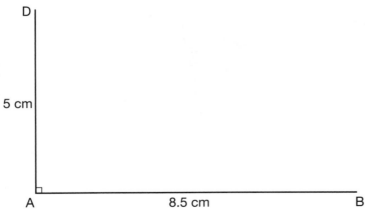

TOTAL ☐

COLLECTING DATA

What you need to know

1 Use and understand tally charts for data collection.

2 Write and criticise questionnaire questions.

3 Understand that data can be affected by the way in which it is collected.

TALLY CHARTS

- A tally chart can be used to record data collected.

  These three tally charts show some data recorded about a class of 30 pupils.

Travel to school	Tally	Frequency
Walk	IIII I	6
Bus	IIII IIII III	13
Car	IIII IIII	9
Cycle	II	2

Days absent last term	Tally	Frequency
0 – 4	IIII IIII IIII	15
5 – 9	IIII IIII	10
10 – 14	IIII	4
15 or more	I	1

Weight, w (kg)	Tally	Frequency
$30 < w \leq 35$	IIII	4
$35 < w \leq 40$	IIII	5
$40 < w \leq 45$	IIII IIII III	13
$45 < w \leq 50$	IIII I	6
$50 < w \leq 55$	II	2

means weight of over 50 kg and up to 55 kg

In the second and third tally charts the data collected has been grouped into class intervals. This is usually done when the data can be lots of different values.

- The data in a tally chart can be interpreted.

  You can see from the tally charts above that the most popular way of getting to school is by bus. You can also work out that 8 pupils weigh over 45 kg (add last two frequencies).

QUESTIONNAIRES

- A 'good' question in a questionnaire is clearly worded and allows the person answering it to choose from a range of responses. 'Tick-box' style answers are often used.

  Here are two 'bad' questions:

  How do you get to school? Tick one box.

  bus ☐   walk ☐

  > Too few answers to choose from.

  How many days were you absent last term? Tick one box.

  0-4 ☐   6-9 ☐   10-14 ☐   15 or more ☐

  > There is a gap between the first two ranges: should be 5–9.

SURVEYS

- When a survey is carried out, it is important to understand that the data collected can be affected by the number of people asked and when and where the data is collected.

- It is important that a big enough **sample** of people is asked. Also, an appropriate range of people should be asked, for example, a mixture of male and female, or different age ranges. The survey should be done at a time and place that makes this possible.

COLLECTING DATA

1 Carolyn has used a tally chart to record the number of hours of sunshine for the first 25 days in June.

Hours of sunshine, t	Tally	Frequency
$0 \leq t < 3$	IIII II	
$3 \leq t < 6$	IIII IIII	
$6 \leq t < 9$	IIII	
$9 \leq t < 12$	III	
$12 \leq t < 15$	I	

Here are the hours of sunshine for the last 5 days in June.

6.7   12.0   2.8   8.4   5.8

(a) Add this data to the tally chart and complete the frequency column.   *1 mark*

(b) How many days in June had **fewer than 6 hours** of sunshine?   *1 mark*

2 Tyrone and Kim each carried out a survey to investigate the number of people in cars passing the school gate. Each time a car passed they recorded the number of people in it.
Here are their data collection sheets.

Whose is the better method?
Tick (✓) Tyrone or Kim.

Tyrone ☐   Kim ☐

Tyrone

Number of people in car

1, 5, 1, 2, 1,
1, 2, 2, 1, 3,
1, 2, 4, 1, 2

Kim

Number of people in car	Tally
1	IIII II
2	IIII
3	I
4	I
5	I

Explain your answer.   *1 mark*

3 Here are three questionnaire questions.
Explain what is wrong with each question.

(a) Please tick one box to show your age range.

under 18 ☐   18–25 ☐   25–35 ☐   35–45 ☐   over 45 ☐

(b) What colour eyes do you have?

blue ☐   brown ☐

(c) How often do you visit the local park?

always ☐   sometimes ☐   occasionally ☐   *3 marks*

4 Sanjay has written a questionnaire to help him find out what people in his town think of the activities on offer at the local leisure centre.
He visits the leisure centre on Tuesday morning at 11 a.m. and asks 10 people to complete the questionnaire.   *2 marks*
Give **two** different reasons why Sanjay's survey may not give very good data.

TOTAL ☐

ROUNDING AND ESTIMATION

What you need to know

1 Round numbers to the nearest unit, ten, hundred, thousand, ...

2 Round decimal numbers to a number of decimal places.

3 Use rounded numbers to estimate answers to calculations.

> **Remember**
> Look at the digit you are rounding to.
> Now look at the digit on its right.
> If it is 4 or less the digit being rounded stays the same.
> If it is 5 or more the digit you are rounding to goes up by 1.

ROUNDING

- In real life it is not always necessary or convenient to use exact numbers. Rounded numbers may be used.

- Numbers can be rounded to different degrees of accuracy, for example, to the nearest thousand, hundred, ten, unit, tenth, hundredth.

Examples Round 17582 to the nearest hundred.

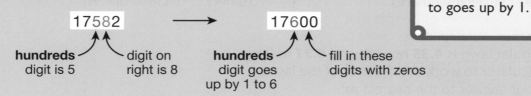

Round 85.42 to the nearest unit (or whole number).

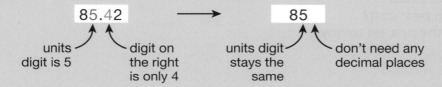

DECIMAL PLACES

- Rounding to a number of decimal places is useful when you end up with an answer on a calculator that has lots of digits after the decimal point.

Example 365 ÷ 47 = 7.765957447...

= 7 . **8** to **1** decimal place (or nearest tenth) | One digit after the decimal point. |

= 7 . **7 7** to **2** decimal places (or nearest hundredth) | Two digits after the decimal point. |

ESTIMATION

- You can estimate the answer to a calculation using rounded numbers.

Example Estimate the answer to 79.62 x 3.273.

Round 79.62 to the nearest ten (80) and 3.273 to the nearest unit (3).

Estimate is 80 x 3 = 240. | This calculation can be done mentally. |

ROUNDING AND ESTIMATION

1 Round these numbers to the degree of accuracy given in brackets.

(a)   45630 (nearest thousand)

(b)   88.6 (nearest ten)

(c)   40.35 (nearest unit)

(d)   4026 (nearest hundred)

(e)   70392 (nearest thousand)

(f)   398.2 (nearest ten)

(g)   0.87 (nearest whole number)

(h)   987 (nearest hundred)

8 marks

2 Round the decimal numbers to the degree of accuracy given in brackets.

(a)   19.763 (1 decimal place)

(b)   13.342 (nearest tenth)

(c)   6.0526 (2 decimal places)

(d)   16.2089 (nearest hundredth)

(e)   4.0921 (1 decimal place)

(f)   0.03442 (2 decimal places)

6 marks

3 A rectangular lawn is **4.35 m** wide and **6.27 m** long.
Use a calculator to work out the area of the lawn,
giving your answer to the nearest **m²**.

2 marks

4 A bag of **7** pears costs **£1.25**.
How much does each pear cost?
Give your answer to the nearest penny
(2 decimal places).

2 marks

5 **Estimate** the answer to this calculation.

(943 ÷ 8.85) + (7.4 x 0.8)

2 marks

6 **Estimate** the area of the painting.
Give the correct units in your estimate.

2 marks

23.6 cm

42.3 cm

TOTAL

USING A CALCULATOR

What you need to know

1. Use a calculator to find powers and roots.
2. Perform complex calculations using a calculator.

POWER AND ROOTS

- You can find squares, cubes and square and cube roots on your calculator.

Square	x^2	To find 3.7^2	enter	3.7	x^2	$=$ 13.69
Cube	x^3	To find 0.8^3	enter	0.8	x^3	$=$ 0.512
Square root	$\sqrt{}$	To find $\sqrt{32}$	enter	$\sqrt{}$	32	$=$ 5.6568...
Cube root	$^3\sqrt{}$	To find $^3\sqrt{7}$	enter	$^3\sqrt{}$	7	$=$ 1.9129...

- Some calculators may not have x^3 and $^3\sqrt{}$. You will need to use the general power key x^y and the general root key $^x\sqrt{}$. Check your user manual.

BRACKETS

- Use the brackets keys $($ $)$ to enter brackets as they are in the calculation.

To work out $38.6 \div (9.4 - 3.72)$ enter the following:

38.6 $\div$ $($ 9.4 $-$ 3.72 $)$ $=$ 6.7957...

ORDER OF OPERATIONS

- Modern calculators use the BODMAS rule to carry out operations in the correct order.

If you enter the calculation $14.3 - 6 \times 1.5^2$

14.3 $-$ 6 $\times$ 1.5 x^2 $=$

the calculator will work out the power first, then do the multiplication and finally the subtraction to give the answer 0.8.

Quick Tip
You need a scientific calculator for KS3 Maths Test Paper 2. Make sure you know how to use your own calculator – there are differences between models.

Remember
If you are asked to calculate something like this: $\dfrac{7 - 2.3}{1.3 + 6}$

remember that it means 'divide the top result by the bottom result'. You will need to enter it as $(7 - 2.3) \div (1.3 + 6)$.

USING A CALCULATOR

1 Find the value of:

(a) 41^2 (b) 1.4^2

(c) 18^2 (d) 5.32^2

(e) 1.5^3 (f) 8.07^2

(g) 11^3 (h) 0.04^3 8 marks

2 Work out each root. Give each answer to 1 decimal place.

(a) $\sqrt{74}$ (b) $\sqrt[3]{9}$

(c) $\sqrt{18}$ (d) $\sqrt[3]{167}$

(e) $\sqrt{8.5}$ (f) $\sqrt[3]{1.56}$ 6 marks

3 Use a calculator to work out each calculation.
Give answers to 2 decimal places where necessary.

(a) $24.3 - 9.75 \div 2.5 + 4.67$

(b) $3.4 \div (9.6 - 2.5)$

(c) $4.6^2 - 2.3^2$

(d) $\sqrt{(6.8 \div 2.2)}$

(e) $\dfrac{2.5}{19.3 - 6.42}$

(f) $\dfrac{3.75 \times 1.06}{5.4 - 2.61}$ 6 marks

TOTAL ⬚

SEQUENCES

What you need to know

1 Describe and explore sequences of numbers and patterns.

2 Find and use the position-to-term formula for a sequence.

NUMBER SEQUENCES

- A sequence is made up of numbers, called **terms**, which are linked by a rule.

Example The rule for a sequence is subtract 3 and the first term is 8.
Give the first few terms.

The sequence is 8, 5, 2, –1, –4, –7, –10, ...

- By studying a sequence you can work out the rule that has been used.

Example Look at the sequence and give the rule.

1000, 100, 10, 1, 0.1, 0.01, ...

The rule for this sequence is divide by 10.

SEQUENCES OF PATTERNS

- There can be rules and formulas for sequences of patterns.

Here is a sequence of patterns made up of squares.

To get the next pattern you add on three squares, one to each 'arm'. You can see that the number of squares needed is linked to the pattern number:

number of squares = 3 x pattern number + 1

This rule can be written using a formula using P as the pattern number and S as the number of squares:

$$S = 3P + 1$$

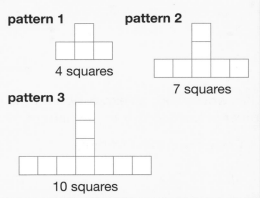

pattern 1 — 4 squares

pattern 2 — 7 squares

pattern 3 — 10 squares

You can use the formula to find out the number of squares in any pattern without drawing the pattern.

For the sequence of patterns above, the 10th pattern will have 3 x 10 + 1 = 31 squares.

POSITION-TO-TERM FORMULA

- For some sequences you can find a position-to-term formula, sometimes called an nth term formula. Let the position of the term in the sequence be called **n**.

Example Find the nth term formula for the sequence 3, 7, 11, 15, ...

position, n	1	2	3	4
term	3	7	11	15 ← go up in 4s but not multiples of 4
	4	8	12	16 ← compare to multiples of 4, formula **4n**
	4 x 1	4 x 2	4 x 3	4 x 4

Notice that each term is 1 less than a multiple of 4

Formula **4n - 1**

SEQUENCES

1 A number sequence has the following rule:

> First term is **46**
> Rule is **subtract 4**

Write down the first five terms of the sequence.

2 Write the missing numbers for each sequence:

(a) 3   ☐   12   24   ☐   96

(b) ☐   –5   ☐   –11   –14   –17

3 The rule for a sequence is:

> Double the previous term and add 3

Work out the missing first two terms of this sequence.

☐   ☐   21   45   93   189

4 Ian is making patterns of hexagons with matchsticks.

pattern 1   **pattern 2**   **pattern 3**

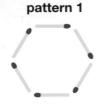  

He has worked out an expression for the number of matchsticks in terms of the number of hexagons, h, in the pattern.

(a)   Circle the correct formula.

$5h$ $5h + 1$ $h + 5$ $5h - 1$ $6h$

(b)   Use the formula you have chosen to work out the number of matchsticks in a pattern which has 15 hexagons.

5 Here is a number sequence: 5, 10, 15, 20, 25, …
The nth term formula for this sequence is **5n**.
Write down the formulas for the sequences below.

(a)   7, 12, 17, 22, 27, …

(b)   –1, 4, 9, 14, 19, …

6 Work out the position-to-term formula for this sequence.

1   5   9   13   17   …

TOTAL ☐

CIRCLES

What you need to know

1 Use formulas for the **circumference** and area of a circle.

THE CIRCLE

r **radius**

d **diameter**

C **circumference** (perimeter)

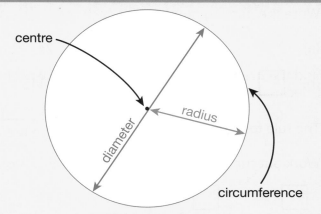

- The diameter is twice the length of the radius so $d = 2r$.
- π is a value used in circle formulas
  - $\pi = 3.141592...$
  - $\pi = 3.14$ to 2 decimal places.
- The value of π is also stored in a scientific calculator – look for it on yours.

> **Remember**
> If you are given the radius of the circle instead of the diameter make sure you **double** it to get the diameter.

CIRCUMFERENCE

- The formula for the circumference of a circle is $C = \pi d$.

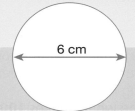

Example $C = \pi \times 6 = 18.85$ cm (answer rounded to 2 decimal places)

Example A wheel has a circumference of 22 cm. Find the diameter of the wheel.

$22 = \pi \times d$

$d = 22 \div \pi = 7.0$ cm (1 decimal place)

> The formula has been used here to find the diameter given the circumference.

AREA

- The formula for the area of a circle is $A = \pi r^2$ (or $\pi \times r \times r$).

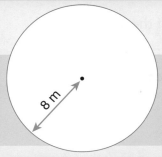

Example $A = \pi \times 8^2 = 201.1$ m^2 (answer rounded to 1 decimal place)

Example A circular rug has an area of 2.5 m^2. Find the radius of the rug.

$2.5 = \pi \times r^2$

$r^2 = 2.5 \div \pi$

$r = \sqrt{0.7957...}$

$r = 0.89$ m (2 decimal places)

> The formula has been used here to find the radius given the area.

> **Remember**
> If you are given the diameter of the circle instead of the radius make sure you **halve** it to get the radius.

CIRCLES

1 Find the **circumference** of each circle. Give your answers in the correct units and to 2 decimal places.

(a)
9 cm

(b)
12 cm

2 marks

2 Find the **area** of each circle. Give your answers in the correct units and to 1 decimal place.

(a)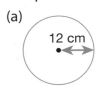
12 cm

(b)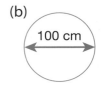
100 cm

2 marks

3 A circle has a **circumference** of **90 cm**.
What is the diameter of the circle?

1 mark

4 A circle has an **area** of **150 m²**.
What is the radius of the circle?

1 mark

5 The front wheel on Kyle's cycle has a diameter of **45 cm**.
Kyle counts the number of turns the front wheel of his cycle makes as he is riding it.
How far has he travelled if the wheel makes **100** turns?

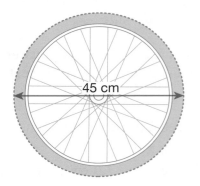
45 cm

2 marks

6 A semi-circular lawn has a radius of 2 m.

(a) Work out the **area** of the lawn.

2 marks

(b) Work out the **perimeter** of the lawn.

2 m

2 marks

TOTAL

What you need to know

1 Find the **mode**, **median**, **mean** and **range** of a set of data.

2 Compare two sets of data using the range and an average (mode, median or mean).

RAW DATA

- Raw data is often given as a list of numbers. The three different averages and the range can be found for a set of raw data.

- The **mode** is the most common value (the value with the highest frequency). It is the easiest to find but for some data sets there may be no mode or more than one mode.

- The **median** is the middle value when the numbers are put in order of size. If there are two middle values then the median is taken as the number half-way between these two values.

- The **mean** is found by adding up all of the data and dividing the total by the number of values.

- The **range** is the difference between the largest and smallest values.

Example Here are the numbers of students in 6 classes in a school.

26   30   28   26   31   27

Find the mode, median, mean and range.

Mode	26	the number 26 appears twice

Median   27.5   26   26   27   ↑   28   30   31

↑ median lies half-way between 27 and 28

Mean   28 $(26 + 30 + 28 + 26 + 31 + 27) \div 6 = 28$

Range   5 $31 - 26 = 5$

- To compare two sets of data, use one of the three averages to compare typical values and the range to compare how spread out the data values are.

FREQUENCY DATA

- A larger data set may be given as a frequency table.

Example The ages and numbers of students taking part in a school play are given in the table.

Find the **modal** and mean ages.

Age (years)	Number of students
13	3
14	8
15	10
16	4

The modal age is 15 as it has the highest frequency.

To find the mean age multiply the numbers in the two columns together, find the total and divide this by the total number of students.

mean $= (13\times3 + 14\times8 + 15\times10 + 16\times4) \div (3 + 8 + 10 + 4)$

$= 365 \div 25 = 14.6$ years old

MODE, MEDIAN, MEAN AND RANGE

1 Find the mode of these shoe sizes.

39   40   38   39   38   41   36   36   38   37   38

1 mark

2 Find the median height for these four students.

165 cm   170 cm   172 cm   168 cm

1 mark

3 Work out the mean and the range for these five weights.

43.1 kg   45.7 kg   38.9 kg   42.3 kg   39.7 kg

2 marks

4 Ellie and Alan are comparing exam marks. The table shows the mean and range for both students.

	Mean	Range
Ellie	73%	10%
Alan	78%	42%

(a)   Compare Ellie and Alan's mean scores.

(b)   What do the ranges tell you about Ellie and Alan's scores?

2 marks

5 Kerry is taking part in a gymnastics competition.
Her performance is marked by six judges.
Here are her scores:

7.8   7.5   8.3   7.8   8.1   9.0

(a)   Use all six scores to work out her mean mark and the range of marks.

2 marks

(b)   In competitions the highest and lowest scores are ignored.
       Use the four remaining scores to work out the new mean and range.

2 marks

(c)   Why do you think the highest and lowest scores are ignored in competitions?

1 mark

6 Here are four number cards.
One of the cards has the number **6** on it.
The other three cards have been placed face down.

The **mode** of the numbers is **6**.
The **mean** is **5** and the **range** is **3**.
What are the numbers on the other three cards?

2 marks

TOTAL

How did you score?

6 or less – try again!
7 – 10 – nearly there!
11 – 13 – well done!

FRACTIONS

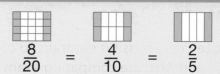

What you need to know

1 Find fractions of shapes.

2 Recognise and make equivalent fractions.

3 Convert between improper fractions and mixed numbers.

EQUIVALENT FRACTIONS

- Equivalent fractions are different fractions that represent the same amount.

- Equivalent fractions can be made by **multiplying** the **numerator** and **denominator** by the same number.

$$\frac{8}{20} = \frac{4}{10} = \frac{2}{5}$$

Examples

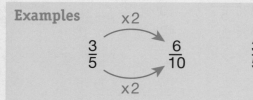

$$\frac{3}{5} \xrightarrow{\times 2} \frac{6}{10}$$

$$\frac{3}{5} \xrightarrow{\times 10} \frac{30}{50}$$

- Some fractions can also be simplified by **dividing** the numerator and denominator by the same number.

Example

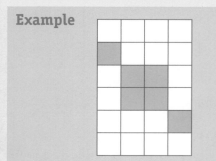

fraction shaded is $\frac{6}{24} \xrightarrow{\div 6} \frac{1}{4}$

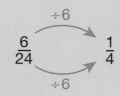

Quick Tip
To compare or order different fractions first change them so that they all have the same denominator.

Example Which is bigger, $\frac{3}{4}$ or $\frac{4}{5}$?

$\frac{3}{4} = \frac{15}{20}$ and $\frac{4}{5} = \frac{16}{20}$ so $\frac{4}{5}$ is bigger.

IMPROPER FRACTIONS

- An improper fraction is a fraction that is greater than 1. The numerator is bigger than the denominator.

- An improper fraction can be written as a mixed number. A mixed number has a whole number part plus a fraction.

$$\frac{13}{8} = \underset{\text{whole}}{\frac{8}{8}} + \frac{5}{8} = 1\frac{5}{8}$$

- A mixed number can also be written as an improper fraction.

$$2\frac{2}{5} = \underset{\text{whole}}{\frac{5}{5}} + \underset{\text{whole}}{\frac{5}{5}} + \frac{2}{5} = \frac{12}{5}$$

FRACTIONS

1 What fraction of each shape is shaded?
Write each fraction in its simplest form.

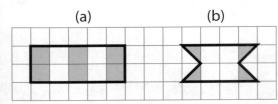

(a)   (b)

2 Write in the missing numbers to complete each equivalent fraction.

(a) $\dfrac{3}{7}$ $=$ $\dfrac{\boxed{}}{21}$ (b) $\dfrac{5}{12}$ $=$ $\dfrac{20}{\boxed{}}$ (c) $\dfrac{10}{25}$ $=$ $\dfrac{\boxed{}}{5}$

3 For each diagram shade the fraction shown.

(a) $\dfrac{1}{8}$ (b) $\dfrac{3}{5}$ (c) $\dfrac{1}{4}$

4 Write each improper fraction as a mixed number.

(a) $\dfrac{8}{5}$ (b) $\dfrac{12}{7}$ (c) $\dfrac{19}{4}$

5 Write each mixed number as an improper fraction.

(a) $3\frac{2}{3}$ (b) $2\frac{1}{5}$ (c) $4\frac{9}{10}$

6 Use an arrow to mark the position of each fraction on the number line.

$\dfrac{3}{4}$ $\dfrac{3}{16}$ $\dfrac{3}{8}$

0                    $\frac{1}{2}$ 1

TOTAL

FRACTIONS, DECIMALS, PERCENTAGES

What you need to know

1 Understand the link between fractions, decimals and percentages.

2 Convert from one to another with and without a calculator.

COMMON EQUIVALENCES

- There are some relationships between fractions, decimals and percentages that are useful to know off by heart. Learn these and use them to work out other equivalences.

Fraction	Decimal	Percentage
$\frac{1}{2}$	0.5	50%
$\frac{1}{4}$	0.25	25%
$\frac{3}{4}$	0.75	75%
$\frac{1}{10}$	0.1	10%
$\frac{1}{100}$	0.01	1%
$\frac{1}{1000}$	0.001	0.1%
$\frac{1}{5}$	0.2	20%
$\frac{1}{20}$	0.05	5%
$\frac{1}{8}$	0.125	12.5%

Examples   Write $\frac{3}{5}$ as a decimal. $\frac{1}{5} = 0.2$ so $\frac{3}{5}$ = 3 x 0.2 = 0.6

Write 0.038 as a percentage.   0.001 = 0.1%   so 0.038 = 38 x 0.1% = 3.8%

CONVERTING BETWEEN FRACTIONS, DECIMALS, PERCENTAGES

- To convert a percentage to a decimal, divide by 100.

43%	43 ÷ 100 = 0.43

- To convert a decimal to a percentage, multiply by 100.

1.7	1.7 x 100 = 170%

- To convert a percentage to a fraction, write the number over 100 and simplify if possible.

36%	$\frac{36}{100} = \frac{9}{25}$

- To convert a fraction to a percentage, multiply by 100 and simplify.

$$\frac{23}{25} \qquad \frac{23}{\cancel{25}_1} \times \overset{4}{\cancel{100}} = 23 \times 4 = 92\%$$

- To convert a fraction to a decimal divide the numerator by the denominator. Some fractions give recurring decimals.

$\frac{9}{16}$ 9 ÷ 16 = 0.5625

$\frac{2}{9}$ 2 ÷ 9 = 0.22222...

Use a calculator here.

- To convert a decimal to a fraction, write the decimal part over 10, 100 or 1000 if it has 1, 2 or 3 decimal places.

0.48 $\frac{48}{100} = \frac{12}{25}$

1.2 $\frac{12}{10} = 1\frac{1}{5}$

Simplify where possible.

FRACTIONS, DECIMALS, PERCENTAGES

1 Without using a calculator write these fractions as decimals.

(a) $\frac{2}{5}$

(b) $\frac{71}{100}$

(c) $\frac{3}{20}$

(d) $\frac{3}{8}$

 4 marks

2 Write these percentages as fractions in their simplest terms.

(a) 5%

(b) 18%

(c) 120%

3 marks

3 Find the percentage and fraction equivalents to these decimals.

(a) $0.39 = \boxed{} \% = \dfrac{\boxed{}}{\boxed{}}$

 2 marks

(b) $0.04 = \boxed{} \% = \dfrac{\boxed{}}{\boxed{}}$

4 Here are two fractions.

$\frac{5}{32}$ $\frac{3}{20}$

Which is the larger fraction? Show your working.
Hint : Use a calculator to convert each fraction to a decimal first.

1 mark

5 (a) Shade in 15% of the diagram.   (b) Shade in 0.625 of the diagram.

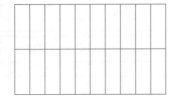 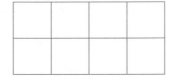

 2 marks

6 Complete each number statement with a **fraction** in its simplest terms.

(a) $0.8 + \boxed{} = 1$

(b) $\boxed{} + 0.27 = 1$

2 marks

TOTAL $\boxed{}$

FUNCTIONS AND MAPPINGS

What you need to know

1 Find inputs and outputs of a **function**.

2 Display a function as points on a graph and in a mapping diagram.

FUNCTIONS

- A **function** takes an input number and maps it to an output number. Some functions have simple rules, for example *multiply by 3*, some are more complex and may involve two or more operations.

FUNCTION MACHINE

- A function can be shown as a 'machine'. The inputs and outputs may be listed in a table.

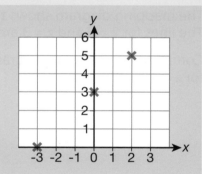

$x \longrightarrow \boxed{\times 2} \longrightarrow \boxed{+ 5} \longrightarrow 2x + 5$

x	$2x + 5$
1	5
4	13
0	5
-5	-5
$\frac{1}{2}$	6

GRAPH OF A FUNCTION

- Inputs and outputs of a function may be plotted as points on a graph.

Example A function maps the number x to the number **$x + 3$**, or $x \rightarrow x + 3$. Plot the three points on a graph.

x	$x + 3$
-3	0
0	3
2	5

- The (x, y) coordinates of each point are a pair of input and output values. Notice that for the function in the example the points lie in a straight line.

MAPPING DIAGRAM

- A function can also be shown as a mapping diagram. Each input on the left maps to an output on the right.

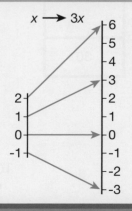

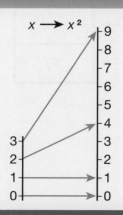

FUNCTIONS AND MAPPINGS

1 Complete the table of inputs and outputs for each function.

(a) $n \longrightarrow n - 6$

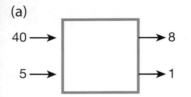

input	output
8	2
15	
4	
	-3

(b) $n \longrightarrow 2n - 7$

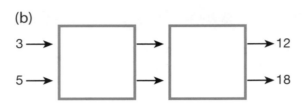

input	output
8	9
10	
	7
2	

2 Write in the missing operations in the function machines.

(a)

40 → [ ] → 8

5 → [ ] → 1

(b)

3 → [ ] → [ ] → 12

5 → [ ] → [ ] → 18

3 (a) Complete the table for the function which maps **x** to **6 – x**.

x	6 - x
0	
2	
4	
6	

(b) Draw a grid from 0 to 8 on both axes. Plot the values in your table as points on your grid.

4 The mapping diagram shows the function $z \longrightarrow 2z - 3$. The lines for $z = 0$ and $z = 3$ are shown.

Complete the mapping diagram by drawing lines for $z = 1$, $z = 2$ and $z = 4$.

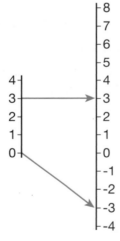

5 Different functions map the number **5** to the number **30**. Complete the tables by writing two **different** functions.

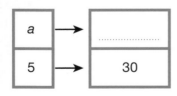

a	....
5	30

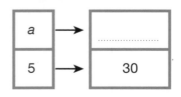

a	....
5	30

TOTAL [ ]

How did you score?

6 or less – try again!
7 – 10 – nearly there!
11 – 14 – well done!

3D SHAPES

What you need to know

1 Identify the properties of some common 3D shapes.

2 Draw a 3D shape on an isometric grid.

3 Recognise 2D representations (plans and elevations, **nets**) of a 3D shape.

COMMON 3D SHAPES

- You should already be able to recognise these 3D shapes: cube, cuboid, sphere, cone, cylinder, pyramids with different bases and prisms.

- Many 3D shapes have flat faces and straight edges which meet at vertices (corners).

- A 3D shape can be described in terms of the number of faces, edges and vertices it has. For example, a triangular prism has 5 faces (two of which are triangles), 9 edges and 6 vertices. In the diagram you can see that the 'hidden' edges are shown as dotted lines.

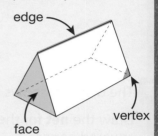

edge — face — vertex

Remember

A **prism** is a 3D shape which always has the same cross-section.

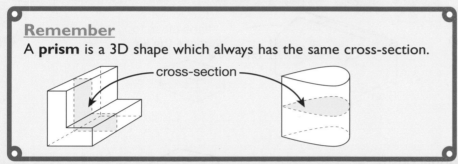

cross-section

ISOMETRIC 3D DRAWINGS

- It is much easier to draw some 3D shapes on an isometric grid. The diagram shows a 3D shape drawn from two different angles.

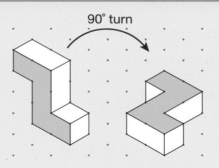

90° turn

Quick Tip

Never use horizontal lines in isometric drawings.

It is a good idea to start by drawing one **vertex** and work from there.

2D REPRESENTATIONS

- One way of representing a 3D shape is to show it as three different 2D views – what it looks like from above (plan), from the front and from the side.

- Another way is to draw the **net** of the shape, what it would look like if folded out flat.

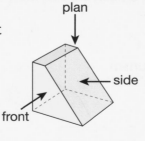

plan — side — front

plan view

front elevation **side elevation**

3D SHAPES

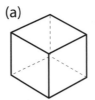

(a)

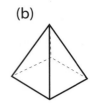

(b)

1 Look at the two 3D shapes. Shape (a) is a cube and (b) is a square based pyramid.
Write down the number of faces, edges and vertices for each shape.

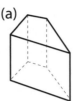

(a)

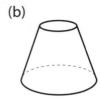

(b)

2 Look at the two 3D shapes. Shape (a) is a prism.
Explain why shape (b) is **not** a prism.

3 The diagram shows a box.

Draw the **net** for the box on squared paper.

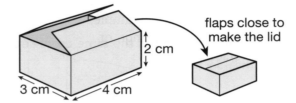

flaps close to make the lid

2 cm

3 cm   4 cm

4 The drawing shows a hexagonal prism.
It is not possible to see all of its faces and edges in this drawing.

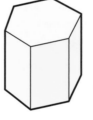

(a) How many of its edges cannot be seen?

(b) How many of its faces cannot be seen?

5 The drawing shows an isometric view of a shape made from 6 cubes – 2 black and 4 white.

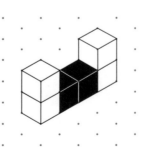

(a) Draw the plan view and front and side elevations of this shape on squared paper.

(b) The six cubes are now used to make a cuboid.
On isometric paper draw a possible cuboid that could be made.

6 This is the net of a triangular prism.
Sketch a **different** net for the same triangular prism.

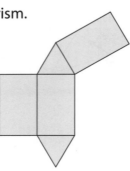

TOTAL [   ]

CHARTS FOR DISPLAYING DATA

What you need to know

1 Display and interpret data in various line graphs, stem and leaf diagrams and bar charts.

USING BAR CHARTS

- You should already be able to read a simple bar chart. In the Test, expect to be given more complicated bar charts to work with.

This bar chart is called a compound bar chart. It has a key to show the different categories. Take care when reading values from it. For example, notice that the number of staff who said 'No' is 50% (= 90% – 40%) not 90%.

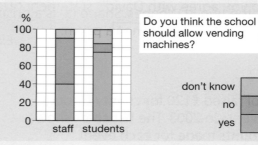

Do you think the school should allow vending machines?

This chart shows ranges of values. For example, you can see that Y7 has the smallest range of heights and the tallest person in Y8 is about 177 cm.

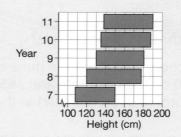

Height ranges of pupils in Years 7 to 11

USING LINE GRAPHS

- Line graphs can be used to present information in an easily read form.

This line graph shows how the average daily temperature in two different cities varied over a year. For example, you can see that at some time during April and October the average temperature was the same for both cities. The highest temperature in city A was about 26°C and occurred in July.

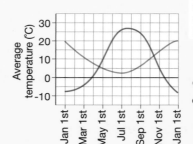

Average daily temperature over a 1 year period

city A ———
city B ———

USING STEM AND LEAF DIAGRAMS

- Stem and leaf diagrams sort and order information.

The diagram shows the time taken by 15 runners to complete one lap of a running track. The key shows you how to read the diagram. For example, the slowest time is 73 seconds and the median time is 62 seconds (the 8th out of 15 values).

Key

4 | 9   means 49 seconds

4	9
5	1 3 3 7 8
6	2 2 3 5 6 7 9
7	0 3

CHARTS FOR DISPLAYING DATA

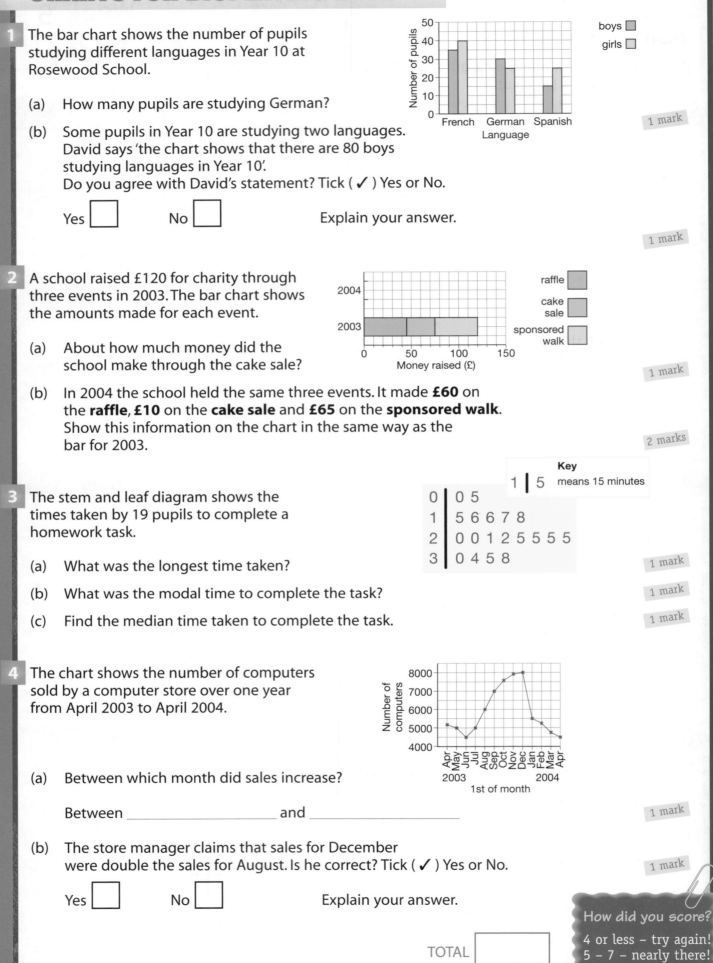

1 The bar chart shows the number of pupils studying different languages in Year 10 at Rosewood School.

(a) How many pupils are studying German?

1 mark

(b) Some pupils in Year 10 are studying two languages. David says 'the chart shows that there are 80 boys studying languages in Year 10'.
Do you agree with David's statement? Tick (✓) Yes or No.

Yes ☐   No ☐   Explain your answer.

1 mark

2 A school raised £120 for charity through three events in 2003. The bar chart shows the amounts made for each event.

(a) About how much money did the school make through the cake sale?

1 mark

(b) In 2004 the school held the same three events. It made **£60** on the **raffle**, **£10** on the **cake sale** and **£65** on the **sponsored walk**. Show this information on the chart in the same way as the bar for 2003.

2 marks

3 The stem and leaf diagram shows the times taken by 19 pupils to complete a homework task.

(a) What was the longest time taken?

1 mark

(b) What was the modal time to complete the task?

1 mark

(c) Find the median time taken to complete the task.

1 mark

4 The chart shows the number of computers sold by a computer store over one year from April 2003 to April 2004.

(a) Between which month did sales increase?

Between _____ and _____

1 mark

(b) The store manager claims that sales for December were double the sales for August. Is he correct? Tick (✓) Yes or No.

1 mark

Yes ☐   No ☐   Explain your answer.

TOTAL ☐

CALCULATIONS WITH FRACTIONS

What you need to know

1 Add, subtract, multiply and divide fractions and mixed numbers.

ADDING AND SUBTRACTING

- This is easy if the fractions have the same denominators.

Example

$$\frac{1}{10} + \frac{3}{10} = \frac{1+3}{10} = \frac{4}{10} = \frac{2}{5}$$

> **Quick Tip**
> Check that you give your answer as a fraction in its simplest form:
> – 'cancel' it to give it in its lowest terms,
> – change an improper fraction to a mixed number.

- If the denominators are different, you need to convert all of the fractions so that they have the same denominators by making equivalent fractions.

Example

$$\frac{7}{8} \xrightarrow{\times 5} \frac{35}{40}$$

$$\frac{7}{8} - \frac{2}{5} \rightarrow \frac{35}{40} - \frac{16}{40} = \frac{19}{40}$$

$$\frac{2}{5} \xrightarrow{\times 8} \frac{16}{40}$$

smallest number that divides exactly by 8 and 5 is 40 – make equivalent fractions with a denominator of 40

MULTIPLYING AND DIVIDING

- To multiply two fractions, multiply the numerators together and multiply the denominators together. You may then need to simplify the fraction to give it in its lowest terms.

Example

$$\frac{2}{5} \times \frac{7}{8} = \frac{2\times7}{5\times8} = \frac{14}{40} = \frac{7}{20}$$

- To divide two fractions, first turn the second fraction upside down, then multiply them as explained above.

Example

$$\frac{4}{9} \div \frac{3}{8} = \frac{4}{9} \times \frac{8}{3} = \frac{32}{27} = 1\frac{5}{27}$$

> **Remember**
> If the question includes any mixed numbers you must first change them to improper fractions before attempting the calculation.
>
> $$1\frac{2}{3} \times \frac{2}{7} = \frac{5}{3} \times \frac{2}{7} = \frac{10}{21}$$

CALCULATIONS WITH FRACTIONS

1 (a) $\frac{7}{11} - \frac{2}{11} =$ (b) $\frac{1}{8} + \frac{5}{8} =$

(c) $\frac{3}{7} + \frac{6}{7} =$ (d) $\frac{8}{15} + \frac{13}{15} =$ 4 marks

2 (a) $\frac{2}{3} - \frac{1}{4} =$ (b) $1\frac{1}{3} + \frac{3}{7} =$

(c) $\frac{3}{4} - \frac{5}{8} =$ (d) $\frac{7}{15} + \frac{4}{5} =$ 4 marks

3 (a) $\frac{7}{9} \times \frac{2}{3} =$

(b) $\frac{6}{7} \times \frac{5}{8} =$

(c) $1\frac{5}{6} \times \frac{3}{11} =$ 3 marks

4 (a) $\frac{3}{8} \div \frac{2}{5} =$

(b) $\frac{7}{10} \div \frac{4}{5} =$

(c) $\frac{3}{4} \div \frac{5}{8} =$ 3 marks

5 In Hightown School **three fifths** of the pupils have a packed lunch.
$\frac{1}{15}$ of the children go home for lunch. The rest of the pupils have a
school lunch.

What fraction of the pupils have a school lunch?   2 marks

TOTAL [ ]

STRAIGHT LINE GRAPHS

What you need to know

1 Use the equation of a straight line to plot and recognise its graph.

2 Use straight line conversion graphs.

EQUATION OF A STRAIGHT LINE

- The general equation of a straight line is $y = mx + c$. The letter m tells you about the gradient (slope) of the line. If it is positive then the line slopes upwards from left to right, if negative it slopes downwards. The letter c gives the intercept of the line – the point at which it crosses the y-axis.

Example A line with the equation $y = 4x - 2$ tells you that the gradient is 4 and the intercept is –2.

- The equation may be used to work out the coordinates of points that lie on the line. The points can be plotted and joined to form a straight line.

Example $y = 2x + 3$

x	-2	0	1	3
y	-1	3	5	9

$2x(-2)+3$ $2 \times 1 + 3$

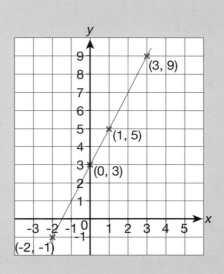

Does the point (20, 42) lie on this line?

You can't tell by looking at the graph as the line is not long enough but you can check using the equation.

Substitute the x-coordinate, 20, into the equation and work out y:

$y = 2 \times 20 + 3 = 43$

The y-coordinate for the point when $x = 20$ is 43, not 42, so the point (20, 42) does not lie on the line.

SOME SPECIAL CASES

- Look out for these special types of straight lines:

$x = 0$ this is the y-axis

$y = 0$ this is the x-axis

vertical lines, for example, $x = -3$ (all the points have an x-coordinate of –3)

horizontal lines, for example, $y = 4$ (all the points have a y-coordinate of 4)

$y = x$ each point has the same x-coordinate as y-coordinate, for example, (–2, –2), (0, 0), (5, 5), …

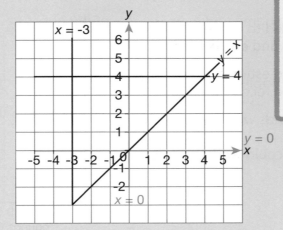

Quick Tip
Many real-life relationships between quantities can be plotted as straight line graphs. You need to be able to interpret these graphs.

57

STRAIGHT LINE GRAPHS

1 Here are some *x* and *y* values for the equation **y = x – 4**.

x	–4	0	7	10
y	–8	–4	3	6

(a) Plot the pairs of values as points on an *x-y* grid (draw a grid from –10 to 10 on each axis). Join the points with a straight line.

1 mark

(b) Does the point (30, 27) lie on the line? Tick (✓) Yes or No.

Yes ☐ No ☐ Explain your answer.

1 mark

2 Complete the table of values for the equation **y = 2x + 5**.

x	0	1	2	3	4	5
y			9			15

2 marks

3 Match each line to its equation.

$y = 2x$

$y = x$

$y = 3$

$x = 3$

$y = x + 3$

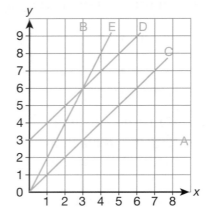

3 marks

4 Circle the **two** equations that give lines with the same gradient.

$y = \frac{1}{2}x + 3$ $y = -\frac{1}{2}x$ $y = 3x + \frac{1}{2}$ $y = \frac{1}{2}x$ $y = x + \frac{1}{2}$

1 mark

5 The following points all lie on the same straight line.

(0, 7) (3, 4) (7, 0) (2, 5)

Circle the equation of the straight line.

$x - y = 7$ $y = 7x$ $x + y = 7$ $y = 7$ $y = x + 7$

1 mark

6 This graph can be used to convert between **pounds** (£) and **euros** (€).

(a) Use the graph to estimate how many euros you would receive for **£40**.

1 mark

(b) How many pounds would you receive for **400 euros**?
Show how you could work this out.

1 mark

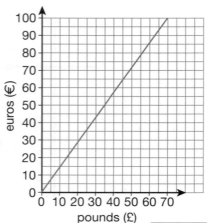

TOTAL ☐

How did you score?

5 or less – try again!
6 – 8 – nearly there!
9 – 11 – well done!

TIME

What you need to know

1 Convert between times in hours, minutes and seconds.

2 Carry out calculations and solve problems involving times.

CONVERTING TIMES

- To convert hours to minutes or minutes to seconds multiply by 60.
- To convert minutes to hours or seconds to minutes divide by 60.

Examples $3\frac{1}{2}$ hours = 3 x 60 + $\frac{1}{2}$ of 60 = 180 + 30 = 210 minutes

240 seconds = 240 ÷ 60 = 4 minutes

> **Remember**
> 0.25 hours does **not** mean 25 minutes.
> 0.25 hours means $\frac{1}{4}$ hour or 15 minutes.
> **But** 00:25 hours means 25 minutes past midnight.

TIME CALCULATIONS

- You cannot add and subtract times in the same way as other numbers. You need to deal with the seconds, minutes and hours separately.

Example Chelsea watches a documentary lasting 56 minutes, a film lasting 1 hour and 38 minutes and a soap lasting 27 minutes. How much TV has she watched in total?

Add minutes together first: 56 + 38 + 27 = 121 minutes

Change this to hours and minutes: 121 = 2 x 60 + 1 = 2 hours 1 minute

Add on any whole hours: 1 hour + 2 hours 1 minute = 3 hours 1 minute

- You may need to work out the difference between two times.

Example A train departs at 14:35 and arrives at its destination at 19:18. How long is the journey? The easiest way to find the difference between these two times is to 'count on' as shown:

14:35   15:00   19:00   19:18

25 mins + 4 hours + 18 mins = 4 hours 43 mins

> **Remember**
> Timetables usually give times in 24 hour clock form.
>
> | 12:00 midnight | 00:00 |
> | 6:00 a.m. | 06:00 |
> | 12:00 noon | 12:00 |
> | 6:00 p.m. | 18:00 |
> | 11:59 p.m. | 23:59 |

TIME

1 Convert these times into the units given.

(a) 4 hours = _____ minutes

(b) 360 seconds = _____ minutes

(c) 2.5 hours = _____ minutes

(d) 1.75 minutes = _____ seconds

(e) 135 minutes = _____ hours _____ minutes

2 Arrange these times in order starting with the shortest.

1 hour 40 minutes   105 minutes   1.5 hours

3 Jo takes the bus into town. It takes **38 minutes**.
She waits **13 minutes** for the coach to take her to the coast.
The journey to the coast takes **2 hours and 45 minutes**.
How long does it take to complete the whole journey?
Give your time in hours and minutes.

4 Here is part of a bus timetable.

	57A	57X
Bradley	11:09	12:25
Little Row	11:14	---
Stanton	11:36	12:48
Greenlaw	12:38	---
Foxton	13:25	14:16

(a) How long does it take the 57A bus to get from Bradley to Foxton?
Give your time in hours and minutes.

(b) The 57X bus takes a shorter time to get from Bradley to Foxton.
How many minutes shorter is this journey?

5 Holly jogs around **2** laps of the running track. Each lap takes her **2 $\frac{1}{2}$** minutes.
She then runs **5** laps of the track, each lap taking her **1 minute
and 45 seconds**.
How long does it take her to complete all seven laps?

TOTAL

VOLUME AND SURFACE AREA OF CUBOIDS

What you need to know

1 Know and use the formula for the **volume** of a cuboid.

2 Find the volume and surface area of a cuboid.

VOLUME

- The **volume** of a cuboid is given by this formula:

  Volume = length x breadth x height

  $V = lbh$

- The units of volume are cubic units such as cm^3 or m^3. When using the formula you must remember that all three **dimensions** must be in the same units. Change them if they are not.

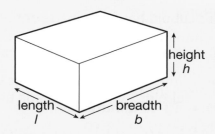

Example Find the volume of the cuboid.

Change 0.2 m into 20 cm, then
V = 30 cm x 30 cm x 20 cm
= 18000 cm^3

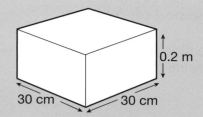

- If you know the volume and two of the three dimensions you can find the third.

Example Find the height of the cuboid.

$$45 = 5 \times 3 \times h$$
$$45 = 15h$$
$$h = \frac{45}{15}$$
$$h = 3$$

Height of cuboid is 3 cm

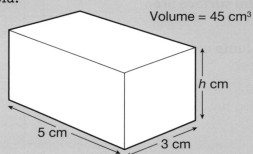

Volume = 45 cm^3

> **Remember**
> Volume and capacity are both measures of the amount of space in a container. Remember that 1 cm^3 = 1 ml.

SURFACE AREA

- A cuboid has six rectangular faces. If you work out the area of each face and add them together you get the surface area of the cuboid.

Example Surface area = 2 x 24 cm^2 + 2 x 30 cm^2 + 2 x 20 cm^2
= 48 cm^2 + 60 cm^2 + 40 cm^2 = 148 cm^2

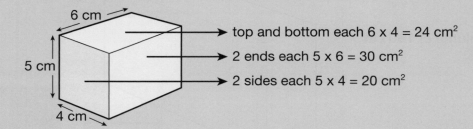

top and bottom each 6 x 4 = 24 cm^2

2 ends each 5 x 6 = 30 cm^2

2 sides each 5 x 4 = 20 cm^2

VOLUME AND SURFACE AREA OF CUBOIDS

1 Work out the volume of each cuboid. Give your answers in cm³.

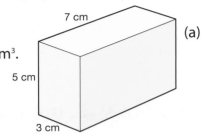 (a)

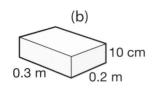 (b)

2 marks

2 This cuboid has been made out of 1 cm³ cubes.

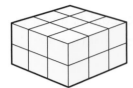

(a) What is the volume of the cuboid?

1 mark

(b) Write down the dimensions of **two different** cuboids that can be made using all the cubes.

2 marks

3 The inside of a small box measures 6 cm by 4 cm by 10 cm. Oliver has some 2 cm cubes.

What is the highest number of cubes he can fit inside the box?

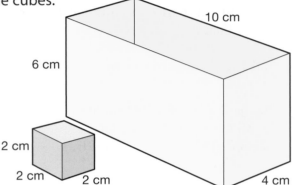

2 marks

4 Here is the net for a cuboid drawn on a cm squared grid.

(a) What is the **total surface area** of the cuboid?

1 mark

(b) What is the **volume** of the cuboid it makes?

1 mark

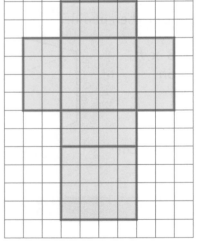

Not actual size

5 A water tank measures 40 cm by 30 cm by 20 cm.

(a) What is the volume of the tank in **cm³**?

1 mark

(b) What is the capacity of the tank in **litres**?

1 mark

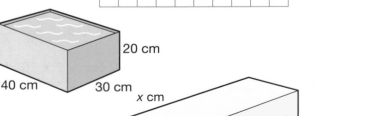

6 The cuboid has a volume of **180 cm³**. Find the value of x.

2 marks

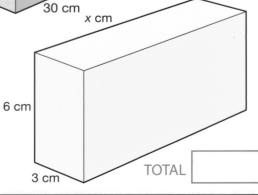

TOTAL ☐

SCATTER DIAGRAMS

What you need to know

1 Plot and interpret data in a scatter diagram.

2 Know what is meant by **correlation**.

DRAWING SCATTER DIAGRAMS

- A scatter diagram is used to investigate the relationship between two quantities. Each pair of values is plotted as a point on the graph. The points are **not** joined.

Example

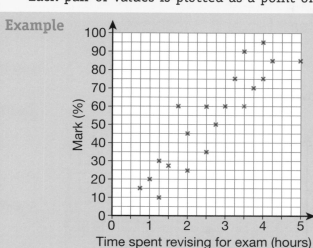

The diagram shows the time spent revising for an exam by 20 pupils and the percentage mark scored in the exam. For example, the pink cross shows one pupil who revised for $3\frac{1}{2}$ hours and scored 60%. The diagram shows that generally the longer the time spent revising the better the mark.

CORRELATION

- The term **correlation** is used when describing the relationship between two quantities.

(a)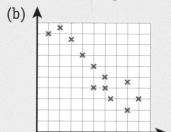

As one quantity increases the other increases – **positive correlation**.

(b)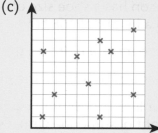

As one quantity increases the other decreases – **negative correlation**.

(c)

There is no link between the two quantities – **no correlation**.

LINE OF BEST FIT

- If there is correlation a line of best fit can be drawn through the centre of the points. This line can then be used to predict other values.

This diagram shows how the value of a particular model of car changes as it gets older. There is negative correlation, that is, the value decreases as the car gets older. The line of best fit can be used to predict that a 3 year model is likely to be worth about £5300.

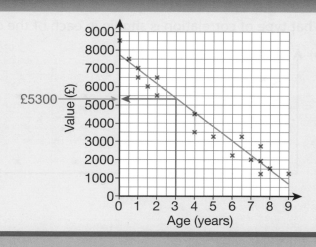

63

SCATTER DIAGRAMS

1 Bethany is investigating whether there is a link between the number of units of gas used in her house and the average monthly temperature.
She has already plotted three points on her scatter diagram.

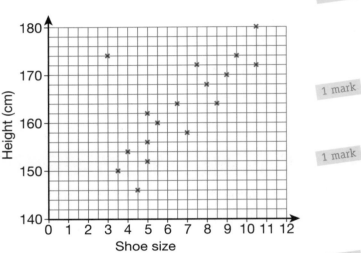

The table contains the rest of her data.

Temperature (°C)	12	7	20	14	18	15
Units of gas	30	45	12	20	15	28

(a) Plot her data as points on the scatter diagram.

2 marks

(b) What type of correlation does the diagram show?
Suggest a reason for your answer.

1 mark

2 The diagram shows the height and shoe size for 17 people.

(a) What does the diagram suggest about shoe size and height?

1 mark

(b) One of the points on the diagram has been plotted incorrectly.
Circle the point you think is incorrect.

1 mark

(c) A further person wishes to add their details to the diagram.
The person has a shoe size of $5\frac{1}{2}$ and a height of 168 cm.

Plot this data as a point on the diagram.

1 mark

(d) Draw a line of best fit on the diagram.

1 mark

(e) Use your line of best fit to estimate the height of someone with a shoe size of 6.

1 mark

(f) Explain why it would not be advisable to use your diagram to predict the height of someone with a shoe size of 2.

1 mark

3 What type of correlation is shown in each of the diagrams?

2 marks

(a)

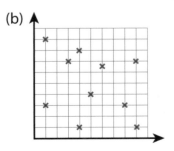

(b)

(c)

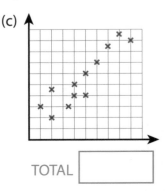

TOTAL [   ]

USING FRACTIONS AND PERCENTAGES

What you need to know

1. Express one quantity as a fraction or percentage of another.
2. Find a fraction or percentage of a quantity.

ONE QUANTITY AS A FRACTION OR PERCENTAGE OF ANOTHER

- It is sometimes useful to give one quantity as a fraction or percentage of a total.

Example   In a class of 32 pupils there are 20 boys.

The fraction of boys in the class is $\frac{20}{32} = \frac{5}{8}$ in its lowest terms.

The percentage of boys can be found by multiplying this fraction by 100.

$\frac{20}{32} \times 100 = \frac{5}{8} \times 100 = 62\frac{1}{2}\%$

- For more difficult quantities you will be able to use a calculator.

Example   Mr Jones puts down £3215 as a deposit on a new car costing £9000.

What is the deposit as a percentage of the price?

$\frac{3215}{9000} \times 100 = 35.7\%$ (rounded to 1 decimal place)

FRACTION OR PERCENTAGE OF A QUANTITY

- You are expected to be able to find a fraction or percentage of a quantity both mentally and using a calculator (for more difficult numbers).

Examples   Find $\frac{3}{10}$ of 75 kg without using a calculator.

First find $\frac{1}{10}$ by dividing by 10   75 ÷ 10 = 7.5 kg

Now multiply this by 3 to get $\frac{3}{10}$ 3 x 7.5 kg = 22.5 kg

Find $\frac{3}{11}$ of 376 kg.

Enter 3 ÷ 11 x 376 = on a calculator to get 102.5 kg (1 decimal place).

Find 24% of £4.50 without using a calculator.

First find 10% by dividing by 10	£4.50 ÷ 10 = 45p
Double this to get 20%	2 x 45p = **90p**
Now find 1% by dividing by 100	£4.50 ÷ 100 = 4.5p
Multiply by 4 to get 4%	4 x 4.5p = **18p**
Add together to get 24%	90p + 18p = **£1.08**

Find 89.5% of £8.56.

Enter 89.5 ÷ 100 x 8.56 = on a calculator to get £7.66 (nearest penny).

USING FRACTIONS AND PERCENTAGES

Do not use a calculator for questions 1 to 4.
You should use a calculator for questions 5 and 6.

1 The table shows the number of girls and boys in three form groups in Year 9 in a school.

Work out the fraction of girls in each form group.
Give your fractions in their lowest terms.

Form group	Boys	Girls
9B	10	20
9C	15	12
9H	14	16

3 marks

2 Jon's marks in three tests are shown below.

Maths   36 out of 40

English   24 out of 30

Science   48 out of 64

Express each of his marks as a percentage.

3 marks

3 (a)   Find $\frac{3}{5}$ of 65 kg.

   (b)   Find $\frac{7}{10}$ of £9.00.

2 marks

4 (a)   Find 30% of £45.

   (b)   Find 13% of 820 km.

2 marks

5 Mrs King earned a salary of **£25 650** last year.
Last year she paid **£5890** in taxes and spent **£10 630** on household bills.
What percentage of her salary was left after she had paid her taxes and household bills?

2 marks

6 A new car is advertised at **£8995**.
A local car dealer decides to reduce the price by **$12\frac{1}{2}$ %** as a special offer.
Work out the special offer price of the car.
Give your answer to the nearest pound.

2 marks

TOTAL [   ]

How did you score?

6 or less – try again!
7 – 10 – nearly there!
11 – 14 – well done!

66

RATIO AND PROPORTION

What you need to know

1 Compare and share out quantities using ratios.

2 Change amounts in proportion to each other.

RATIO

- A ratio is used to compare one quantity with another.

Example Over a period of 6 weeks there were 10 wet days and 32 dry days.

Ratio of wet to dry days   10 : 32

Simplify by dividing by 2   5 : 16

This ratio can also be given as a unit ratio by dividing so that one side is equal to 1.

Divide by 5   1 : $\frac{16}{5}$

1 : 3.2

This means that for every wet day there were 3.2 dry days.

- A quantity can be shared in a given ratio.

Example Three friends share a prize of £1200 in the ratio 2 : 3 : 5.

Number of 'shares' is given by   2 + 3 + 5 = 10

Each 'share' is worth   £1200 ÷ 10 = £120

Multiply each part of the ratio by the share 2 x £120 : 3 x £120 : 5 x £120

£240 : £360 : £600

PROPORTION

- Quantities that are in proportion to each other can be increased or decreased by multiplying or dividing them all by the same number.

Example How much flour would be needed to make 18 biscuits?

Shortbread Recipe

50 g sugar
100 g butter
150 g flour

makes 12 biscuits

150 g of flour is needed for 12. 12 is multiplied by 1.5 to get 18 so multiply the amount of flour by 1.5 to get 225 g.

How much flour is needed if 35 g of sugar is used?

Dividing the amount of sugar and flour in the recipe by 50 shows that for every 1 g of sugar 3 g of flour is needed.

So if 35 g of sugar is used then 35 x 3 = 105 g of flour is needed.

RATIO AND PROPORTION

1 Simplify each ratio giving the final ratio in its lowest terms.

    (a)   16 : 12

    (b)   48 : 32

    (c)   10 : 15 : 35

3 marks

2 **95** students out of a class of **120** passed an exam.

    (a)   Write the number of students who failed compared to the number who passed as a ratio in its lowest terms.

1 mark

    (b)   Now write the ratio of students who failed to students who passed in the form 1 : n.

1 mark

3 A garden has a total area of **81 m²**. The garden is divided into a patio, a lawn and flower beds in the ratio **2 : 3 : 4**.
Work out the area of the **patio**.

1 mark

4 Max makes a milk shake by mixing 2 measures of fruit syrup to 7 measures of milk.
How much **syrup** does he need to use with **350 ml of milk**?

1 mark

5 Jack is using this recipe for making cheese scones.

Cheese Scones (makes 8 scones)

160 grams flour
30 grams margarine
80 grams cheese
1 egg
30 ml milk

    (a)   How many grams of margarine would he need to make **12** scones?

1 mark

    (b)   Jack uses the recipe with **120 grams** of **flour**.
How many grams of **cheese** will he need?

1 mark

6 A garden consists of a lawn surrounded by a path made from square paving stones.

    (a)   Show that the ratio of the area of the lawn to the area of the path is **5 : 9**.

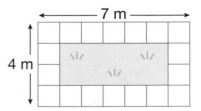

1 mark

    (b)   What fraction of the garden is **lawn**?
Give your fraction in its simplest terms.

1 mark

TOTAL

How did you score?

5 or less – try again!
6 – 8 – nearly there!
9 – 11 – well done!

What you need to know

1 Solve an **equation** using an algebraic method.

2 Solve an equation using a method of trial and improvement.

USING ALGEBRA

- An **equation** may be solved by rearranging it until the letter is left on its own on one side of the equation. Remember that whatever you do to one side of the equation you must also do to the other side.

Example	Solve	$4m - 3 = 13$
	add 3 to both sides	$4m = 13 + 3$
	simplify	$4m = 16$
	divide both sides by 4	$m = 4$

> **Remember**
> Solutions to equations can also be fractions or negative numbers.

Example	Solve	$3q + 2 = 7$
	subtract 2 from both sides	$3q = 7 - 2$
	simplify	$3q = 5$
	divide both sides by 3	$q = \frac{5}{3}$
		$q = 1\frac{2}{3}$

- Some equations may require more steps to solve them.

Example	Solve	$5k + 8 = 2k + 10$
	subtract 2k from both sides	$5k - 2k + 8 = 10$
	subtract 8 from both sides	$5k - 2k = 10 - 8$
	simplify	$3k = 2$
	divide both sides by 3	$k = \frac{2}{3}$

TRIAL AND IMPROVEMENT

- Some equations cannot be solved by rearranging. A method of trying different numbers in place of the letter is carried out until the sides of the equation balance as closely as possible.

Example Solve $n^2 - n = 60$.

Record your trials in a table.

n	$n^2 - n$	Comment
9	$9^2 - 9 = 72$	too high
8	$8^2 - 8 = 56$	too low
8.5	$8.5^2 - 8.5 = 63.75$	too high
8.3	$8.3^2 - 8.3 = 60.59$	too high
8.2	$8.2^2 - 8.2 = 59.04$	too low

You can see that the last two results are very close to 60 so n must lie between 8.2 and 8.3. Further trials would result in a more accurate value for n.

EQUATIONS

1 Solve each equation.

(a) $y + 2y + 4y = 21$ 1 mark

(b) $3k + 5 = 23$ 1 mark

(c) $5m - 8 = 22$ 1 mark

(d) $7 + 4t = 10$ 1 mark

(e) $4q + 5 = 1$ 1 mark

2 Solve each equation.

(a) $8a + 4 = 3a + 19$ 2 marks

(b) $6q - 12 = 8 + 2q$ 2 marks

(c) $9t + 2 = 3t + 5$ 2 marks

3 The perimeter of the triangle is **47 cm**.

(a) Show that the perimeter of the triangle can be written as the equation **$8a + 7 = 47$**.

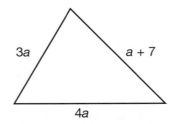

1 mark

(b) Solve the equation to find the value of **a**. 1 mark

4 Here is an equation.
$$x^2 + x = 38$$
Continue the table to find two values, to 1 decimal place, that x lies between.

x	$x^2 + x$	Comment
5	30	too small
6		
5.5		

x lies between _____ and _____.

2 marks

TOTAL

How did you score?
6 or less – try again!
7 – 12 – nearly there!
13 – 15 – well done!

What you need to know

1   Use angle facts to find the sizes of unknown angles.

ANGLE FACTS

- There are a number of special relationships between angles made from straight lines. If you know the sizes of some angles in a diagram it may be possible to work out the sizes of other angles using these facts.

- Angles on a straight line add up to 180°.

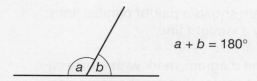

$a + b = 180°$

- Angles at a point add up to 360°.

$a + b + c + d = 360°$

- Vertically opposite angles are equal.

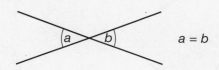

$a = b$

> See the 2D shapes section (pages 13–14) for angle facts about triangles, quadrilaterals and polygons.

- The exterior angle of a triangle is equal to the sum of the two interior opposite angles.

$c = a + b$

PARALLEL LINE ANGLES

- Corresponding angles are equal (look for the letter F).
- Alternate angles are equal (look for the letter Z or N).
- Interior angles add up to 180° (look for the letter U or C).

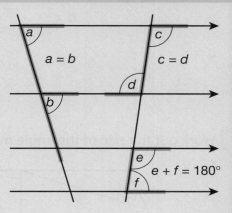

$a = b$ $c = d$

$e + f = 180°$

Example   ABCD is a rectangle. Find angle a.

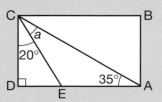

> **Quick Tip**
> In some cases you may need to work out other angles in the diagram before you work out the one you have been asked to find.

angle BCA = 35°
(alternate angles)

so $a = 90° - 35° - 20° = 35°$

ANGLES

1 Work out the size of the angle marked by a letter in each diagram.

          (a)   (b)   (c)

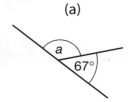   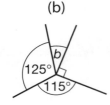   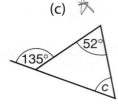

3 marks

2 The diagram shows a pair of parallel lines crossed by a straight line.

(a) On the diagram, mark with crosses a pair of angles that are the same size.

(b) On the diagram, mark with small squares a pair of angles that add up to 180°.

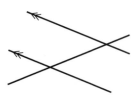

2 marks

3 Work out the size of each angle marked by a letter in the diagram.

a =   *b* =

c =   *d* =

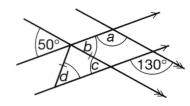

3 marks

4 Find the size of the angle *k* in the diagram.

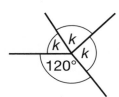

1 mark

5 Work out the size of each angle marked by a letter in the diagram.

a =   *b* =

c =

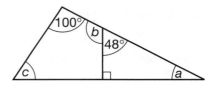

3 marks

6 Work out the size of the angle marked *a* in the diagram.

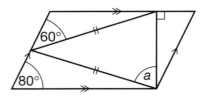

3 marks

TOTAL

PIE CHARTS

What you need to know

1 Interpret data and draw conclusions from pie charts.

2 Construct a pie chart.

INTERPRETING PIE CHARTS

• A pie chart is useful for comparing categories and is particularly good at showing each category as a part of the total. Each sector (slice) represents a different **frequency**. By recognising the fraction of each sector you can work out, or estimate, the frequency for each sector.

This pie chart shows the hot drinks sales for a vending machine. A total of 100 drinks are represented.

You can see that $\frac{1}{2}$ of the chart represents coffees and $\frac{1}{4}$ represents hot chocolates. This works out at 50 (half of 100) cups of coffee and 25 (quarter of 100) hot chocolates. It is not possible to tell exactly how many soups were sold but you could estimate this to be about 9 or 10.

INTERPRETING PIE CHARTS WITH ANGLES

• If you know the angle of each sector you can work out the frequency for each category.

This pie chart shows how 30 pupils travel to school.

First work out how many degrees are used to represent **one** pupil.

360° ÷ 30 = 12° per pupil

Now divide each sector angle by 12 to find out the frequency for each category.

Bus: 204° ÷ 12° = **17**

Car: 96° ÷ 12° = **8**

Walk: 60° ÷ 12° = **5**

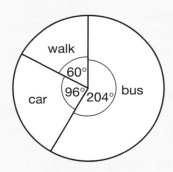

CONSTRUCTING PIE CHARTS

• To construct a pie chart you need to calculate the sector angles.

A pie chart can be constructed to show the results of 24 matches for a football team. Start by working out the number of degrees needed to represent **one** match (360° ÷ 24 = 15° per match) then multiply this by the number of matches in each category.

Now divide a circle into the three sectors using a protractor to draw the angles.

Result	Number of games	Size of angle
Win	7	15° x 7 = 105°
Lose	3	15° x 3 = 45°
Draw	14	15° x 14 = 210°

> **Quick Tip**
> Be careful! When comparing two pie charts, **don't** assume that they both show the same numbers of items.

PIE CHARTS

1 The pie chart shows the different amount of each fruit in a **120 gram** serving of fruit salad.

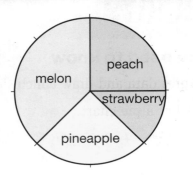

(a) What fraction of the fruit salad are strawberries? 1 mark

(b) How many grams of melon are there in the serving? 1 mark

2 Mr Lyons has drawn a pie chart to show the grades he awarded to some of his students.

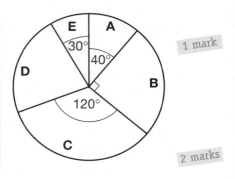

(a) What is the size of the angle for the sector marked **D**? 1 mark

(b) Eight students were awarded a grade **A**. Use this information to work out the number of students achieving the other grades. Complete the table.

Grade	Number of students
A	8
B	
C	
D	
E	

2 marks

3 In a survey 100 people were asked how many portions of fruit and vegetables they typically eat each day. A pie chart was used to display the results.

Complete the table to show how many people are represented in each category.

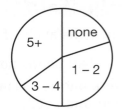

Number of servings	Angle	Number of people
none	72°	
1–2	108°	
3–4	54°	
5+	126°	

3 marks

4 Fazrul asked 180 pupils 'How much TV did you watch last night?' His results are shown in the table.

Use Fazrul's results to draw a pie chart.

Time spent watching TV last night	Number of pupils
less than 2 hours	48
2–4 hours	106
more than 4 hours	26

3 marks

5 A museum wants to compare the visitors it received over three days. The curator has drawn three pie charts, one for each day.

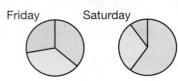
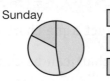

(a) On which day were over half of the visitors children? Tick **one** box.

Friday ☐   Saturday ☐   Sunday ☐   can't tell ☐   1 mark

(b) Which day had the greatest number of visitors? Tick **one** box.

Friday ☐   Saturday ☐   Sunday ☐   can't tell ☐   1 mark

TOTAL ☐

How did you score?
6 or less – try again!
7 – 10 – nearly there!
11 – 13 – well done!

SYMMETRY, REFLECTIONS AND ROTATIONS

What you need to know

1 Recognise line and rotational symmetry in 2D shapes.

2 Reflect a shape about a mirror line.

3 Rotate a shape about a point.

SYMMETRY

• Shapes can have line or rotational symmetry. Some shapes have both but some have no symmetry at all.

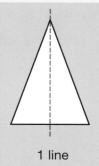 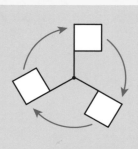 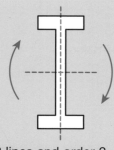 

| 1 line | order 3 | 2 lines and order 2 | no symmetry |

> **Remember**
> The order of symmetry is the number of times the shape looks the same through one full turn.

REFLECTION

• A shape reflected in a mirror line produces an image that is the same distance from the mirror line as the shape.

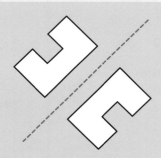 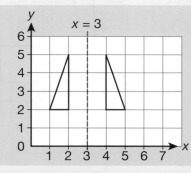

> **Quick Tip**
> If the Test contains a question on symmetry you will be given tracing paper and you may ask for a mirror to help you.

ROTATION

• A shape can be rotated about a given point (either on the shape itself or distant from the shape) and through a given angle and direction.

180° rotation about different points

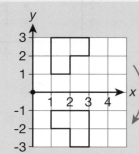

90° clockwise about (0, 0)

SYMMETRY, REFLECTIONS AND ROTATIONS

1 State the number of lines of symmetry and the order of rotational symmetry for each shape.

(a) (b)

2 marks

2 Reflect each shape in the dotted line.

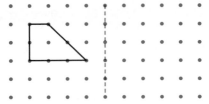 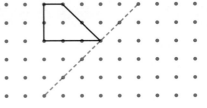

2 marks

3 A rhombus is shown on dotted paper.

Draw **two** more rhombuses of the **same** size to make a shape that has an order of rotational symmetry of 6.

1 mark

4 On the grid draw the reflection of the shape in the line $y = 3$.

Write down the coordinates of the point A on the **reflected** shape.

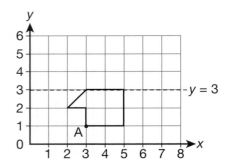

2 marks

5 The shape labelled A on the grid has been rotated to give shape B.

Complete the description of the rotation that has taken place.

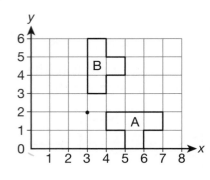

Shape A has been rotated through _____ ° in a _____

direction about the point (_____ , _____). 1 mark

TOTAL _____

TRANSLATION AND ENLARGEMENT

What you need to know

1. Translate a shape on a grid.
2. Recognise and use **congruent** shapes.
3. Enlarge a shape about a point and for a given **scale factor**.

TRANSLATION

- A shape can be translated by moving it sideways or up/down or a combination of both.

move 3 squares to the left and 2 squares down

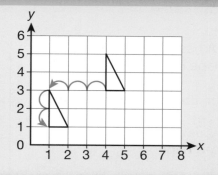

TESSELLATIONS

- If a shape is reflected, rotated or translated it stays the same shape and size. Its orientation and position change.

- These shapes are all **congruent**, that is identical.

- Some shapes can be fitted together to make a pattern without any gaps. This is called a **tessellation**.

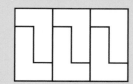 

ENLARGEMENT

- A shape can be enlarged about a point, called the centre of enlargement, and by a given **scale factor**.

Notice that the lengths in the enlarged shape (B) are 3 times the lengths of those in the original shape (A). Shape B is also 3 times the distance from the centre of enlargement. Shapes A and B are not congruent but **similar** (same shape but different sizes).

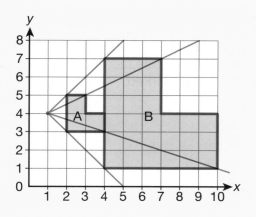

77

TRANSLATION AND ENLARGEMENT

1 Look at the shapes on the dotted grid.

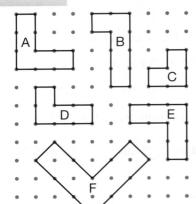

Complete the sentences.

(a) Shapes _____ and _____ are congruent.

1 mark

(b) Shape _____ is an enlargement of shape _____ .

1 mark

2 Shape A has been translated to give shape B.

Describe the translation of A to B.

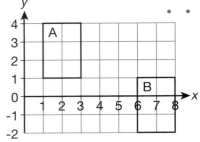

1 mark

3 The diagram shows triangle ABC.

Triangle ABC is enlarged by a scale factor of **4**. Complete the dimensions of the **enlarged** shape.

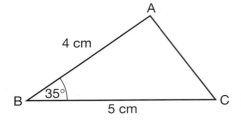

Length of side AB _____ cm

Length of side BC _____ cm

Size of angle B _____ °

2 marks

4 A shape and its enlargement are shown on the grid.

Draw lines on the diagram to find the centre of enlargement. Write down the coordinates of the centre of enlargement.

(_____ , _____)

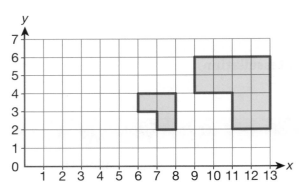

1 mark

5 A triangle is shown on the grid.

On the grid, draw the enlargement of the triangle by a scale factor of **2** about the point marked.

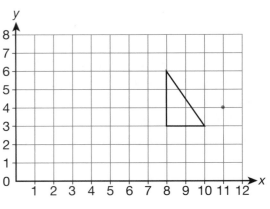

2 marks

TOTAL [   ]

How did you score?

3 or less – try again!
4 – 6 – nearly there!
7 – 8 – well done!

USING NUMBER AND ALGEBRA FACTS

What you need to know

1 Use given number and algebra facts to find others.

USING NUMBER FACTS

- There will be questions in the Tests that check your understanding of numbers and number operations.

Example Here is the 37 times table.

Use these multiplication facts to work out:

(a) 16 x 37

10 x 37 = 370 and 6 x 37 = 222

so 16 x 37 = 370 + 222 = 592

(b) 666 ÷ 37

Know that 9 x 37 = 333 so work out that 18 x 37 = 666

Now use the fact that ÷ is the inverse of x to get 666 ÷ 37 = 18

(c) 4 x 74

Recognise that 74 is 2 x 37 so rewrite 4 x 74 as 4 x 2 x 37 which is the same as 8 x 37 so 4 x 74 = 8 x 37 = 296

1 x 37 = 37
2 x 37 = 74
3 x 37 = 111
4 x 37 = 148
5 x 37 = 185
6 x 37 = 222
7 x 37 = 259
8 x 37 = 296
9 x 37 = 333
10 x 37 = 370

Example A fraction may be written as a decimal, for example: $\frac{4}{25} = 0.16$

(a) Use this fact to write $\frac{29}{25}$ as a decimal.

Write $\frac{29}{25}$ as a mixed number $\qquad 1\frac{4}{25}$

Now write as a decimal recognising that $\frac{4}{25}$ is the given fraction $\quad 1.16$

(b) Use this fact to write 0.32 as a fraction.

Recognise that 0.32 = 2 x 0.16 so 0.32 as a fraction is 2 x $\frac{4}{25}$ = $\frac{8}{25}$

USING ALGEBRA FACTS

- Equations can also be adapted using number operations.

Example Here are two equations: $3a - 2b = 7 \qquad 10c + 6d = 30$

Use the equations to complete the following:

(a) $9a - 6b = \ldots\ldots\ldots$

Obviously use the first equation (it has a and b in it).

Notice that the terms are 3 times those in the given equation so the answer must also be multiplied by 3 to give 21.

(b) $\ldots\ldots\ldots + \ldots\ldots\ldots = 15$

Use the second equation as it has a + in it.

Notice that 15 is half of 30 so the terms must also be halved, that is $5c$ and $3d$.

(c) $3a - 7 = \ldots\ldots\ldots$

Notice that this is a rearranged version of the first equation. Answer must be $2b$.

USING NUMBER AND ALGEBRA FACTS

Do not use a calculator for any of these questions.

1 Here are some multiplication facts.

Use these multiplication facts to work out each calculation.
Show your working each time.

(a) 13 x 52

(b) 468 ÷ 52

(c) 12 x 26

1 x 52 =	52
2 x 52 =	104
3 x 52 =	156
4 x 52 =	208
5 x 52 =	260
6 x 52 =	312
7 x 52 =	364
8 x 52 =	416
9 x 52 =	468
10 x 52 =	520

1 mark

1 mark

2 marks

2 Fractions may be written as decimals.

$\frac{13}{40} = 0.325$ $\frac{31}{16} = 1.9375$

(a) Write $\frac{15}{16}$ as a decimal.

(b) Write 0.975 as a fraction.

1 mark

1 mark

3 The table shows some percentages of £5 and £40.

	2%	5%	10%
£40	80p	£2	£4
£5	10p	25p	50p

Use the figures in the table to work out the following:

(a) 15% of £40

(b) 32% of £5

(c) £2.25 is 5% of how much?

(d) What percentage of £40 is £2.40?

1 mark

1 mark

1 mark

1 mark

4 Find the number half way between 18 x 34 and 22 x 34.
Show your working.

2 marks

5 Here are two equations:
        $4j + 2k = 10$ $2k = j + a$

(a) Use one of the equations to find the value of this expression.

    $2j + k =$ _____

1 mark

(b) Use the equations to show that $5j + a = 10$.

1 mark

TOTAL [ ]

What you need to know

1   Use shape facts to solve shape and space problems.

USING SHAPE FACTS

- There will be questions in the Tests that check your knowledge of shapes and spatial awareness. These questions may link together different aspects of shape, and possibly other, work. Sometimes they test how good you are at visualising shapes.

Example   Here is a paper circle.

If it is folded along the dotted line it makes a different shape.

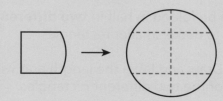

(a) Another paper circle has been folded to make a different shape. Draw dotted lines on the circle to show the folds that must have been made.

The red dotted lines show the folds required.

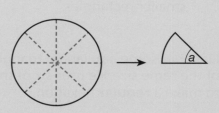

(b) Here is another paper circle. If it is folded along the dotted lines it makes the shape shown. What is the size of the angle marked on this shape?

The folds divide the shape into eight equal parts. The angle for each part is the same size. The size of the angle is 360° ÷ 8 = 45°.

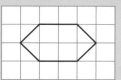

This question tests your ability to visualise shapes made from others and your knowledge of symmetry and angle facts.

Example   A hexagon is shown in the grid. It has an **area** of **6 cm²**.

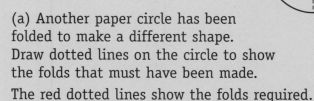

(a) Draw the same hexagon **enlarged** by a **scale factor of 2** on the grid.

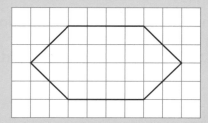

(b) Complete and simplify the ratio of the areas of the two hexagons.

        6 : ...24...
   ...1... : ...4....

This question combines some shape and number work. It tests whether you can enlarge a shape, work out an area by counting squares and then use and simplify ratios.

USING SHAPE AND SPACE FACTS

1 (a) A square piece of paper is folded along the dotted line. Two shapes are cut from it. The paper square is then unfolded.

Draw how the paper looks now.

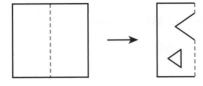

1 mark

(b) Another square piece of paper is folded along the two dotted lines. One shape is cut from it. The paper square is then unfolded.

Draw how the paper looks now.

1 mark

2 A rectangular piece of paper measures 30 cm by 20 cm.

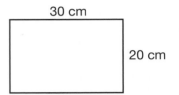

It can be folded in half in **two different** ways to make smaller rectangles.

(a) Draw and label the length and width of the two different rectangles.

1 mark

(b) Work out the perimeter of each of the smaller rectangles.

1 mark

3 Liam has some equilateral triangles of the same size. He uses six of them to make a **regular** hexagon.

(a) Work out the size of angle **a**.

1 mark

(b) Regular hexagons tessellate – they make patterns without gaps.

Explain why regular hexagons tessellate.

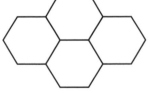

1 mark

4 A paper triangle is folded along the dotted line. The shape it makes is shown on the grid.

Another identical paper triangle is folded along a **different** dotted line.
Draw the shape it makes on the grid.

1 mark

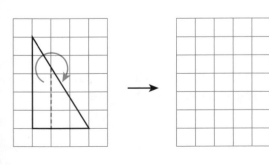

TOTAL [ ]

USING DATA AND PROBABILITY

What you need to know

1   Use probability and data to solve data handling problems.

USING DATA AND PROBABILITY FACTS

- There will be questions in the Tests that check your ability to work with data presented in the form of tables, diagrams and charts. These questions may link together different aspects of handling data and may be linked with probability. The questions may also test how well you understand the problems that can arise in collecting and using data in real-life situations.

Example   Two shops that sell electronic goods have presented recent sales data in the form of charts. The charts compare the sales of DVD players, digital cameras and MP3 players. Digisounds has shown its data in the form of a bar chart. Techmart has shown its data in the form of a pie chart.

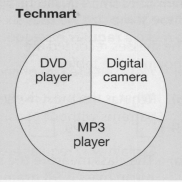

(a) Estimate how many **more** digital cameras than DVD players were sold by **Digisounds**.

Reading the bar chart shows that digital camera sales were about 3400 compared to 2300 DVD players.

1100 more digital cameras were sold. An answer of between 1000 and 1200 would be accepted.

(b) Which shop sold more DVD players? Tick your answer.

Digisounds ☐   Techmart ☐   Can't tell ☐

Explain your answer.

The 'can't tell' box should be ticked and a correct explanation must be given to be awarded the mark.

It is possible to read off the sales from the bar chart for Digisounds. However, the Techmart pie chart only compares the products sales – no numbers are given.

Example   Billy and Abena each had a different dice which they rolled 60 times. They both recorded the number of times each score occurred.

	1	2	3	4	5	6
Billy	9	8	12	12	8	11
Abena	6	6	4	5	8	31

Which person is using a **biased** dice? Tick Billy or Abena.

Billy ☐   Abena ☐

Explain you answer.

Abena should be ticked and a suitable explanation given for the mark.

On a fair dice you would expect to get about the same number for each score on the dice. Abena's dice must be biased because the number 6 occurs about half of the time whilst the other scores only occur a few times each.

USING DATA AND PROBABILITY

1 A fish and chip shop records the number of fish sold on a Friday.
The results are recorded in a two-way table.

	Small	Medium	Large
Cod	30	45	6
Haddock	21	27	8
Sole	9	4	—

(a) How many more cod than haddock were sold?

(b) The manager of the fish and chip shop uses the data to predict the likely number of fish that will be sold every Friday.
What is the probability of a person buying a **small cod?**
Give your answer as a fraction in its simplest terms.

(c) **15** people come into the shop at lunchtime.
Estimate how many **small haddock** the shop is likely to sell.

3 marks

2 Oliver and Robert carried out a survey about shopping in their local town in which they asked 100 people about car parking.
Oliver carried out his survey on a Tuesday morning at 9 a.m. Robert carried out his survey on a Saturday afternoon at 1 p.m.
Here are their results.

Give a possible reason why their results are quite different.

1 mark

Do you think there are enough car parking spaces in town?

Yes ☐   No ☐   Don't know ☐

	Yes	No	Don't know
Oliver	39	8	3
Robert	20	25	5

3 The mass of an apple was measured by 14 pupils using these scales:

The masses recorded are shown in the table.

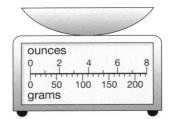

Mass (grams)	Number of pupils
4	5
100	2
110	4
120	3

(a) What is the most likely mass of the apple? Tick **one** box.

4g ☐   100g ☐   110g ☐   120g ☐   Explain your choice.   *1 mark*

(b) The class measure the masses of **50** different apples and work out that the mean mass is **90 grams**. What is the **total mass** of the apples? Give your answer in **kilograms**.

2 marks

4 A spinner is divided into 4 sections numbered 1, 2, 3 and 4.
The spinner is spun 160 times. The frequency of each score is recorded and the results are shown in the bar chart.

(a) What is the probability of landing on **3**?
Give your answer as a fraction in its simplest form.

1 mark

(b) **Use the results in the bar chart** to draw what the spinner could look like. Divide it into four sections and number each one.

2 marks

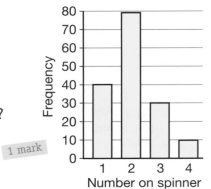

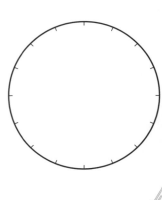

TOTAL ☐

How did you score?

4 or less – try again!
5 – 7 – nearly there!
8 – 10 – well done!

PRACTICE TEST

Allow yourself **1 hour** for this test. There are **60 marks** available.
You will need: pen, pencil, eraser, ruler, tracing paper or mirror, calculator.
You **must not** use a calculator unless the question says you may.

1. Work out the missing numbers.

(a) 338 + ☐ = 1066

1 mark

(b) ☐ x 13 = 117

1 mark

2. Here is the net of a solid shape on a square grid.

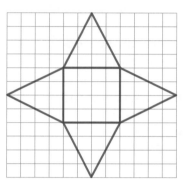

(a) Which solid shape could be made from this net?

_____

1 mark

(b) What is the **area** of the net?

_____ squares

1 mark

3. Here are four number cards. ☐2☐ ☐7☐ ☐6☐ ☐4☐

(a) Use all four number cards once to
make the number **closest to 5000**.

☐☐☐☐

1 mark

(b) Use all four number cards once to
complete the addition to give the
largest possible answer.

☐☐ + ☐☐

1 mark

4. Look at this shape made from four
centimetre cubes.
One side has been coloured grey.
The shape is rotated through **90°**
in a **clockwise** direction so that
the grey side is now the base.

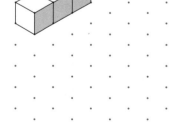

(a) Draw the rotated shape on
the dotted grid.

2 marks

(b) The four centimetre cubes are now used to make a cuboid.
What is the surface area of the cuboid?

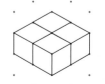

_____ cm²

1 mark

85

5. (a) The rule for this number chain is **divide by 10**.
Fill in the two missing numbers.

4000 → 400 → 40 → _____ → _____

(b) The rule for this number chain is **multiply by 4**.
Fill in the two missing numbers.

_____ → 20 → 80 → _____ → 1280

6. Here is the knob used to set different programs on a washing machine. Each program is given a letter. The letters are equally spaced around the dial.

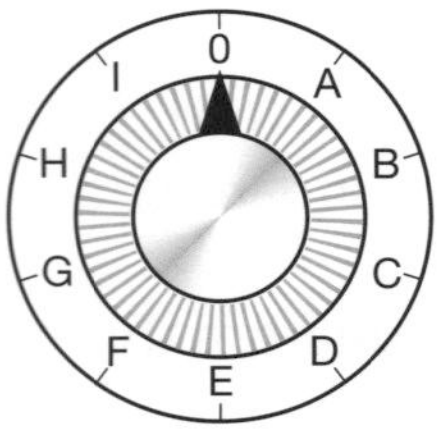

(a) What is the size of the angle between programs **E** and **O**? _____ °

(b) What is the size of the angle between programs **F** and **H**? _____ °

7. A car is joined to a trailer using a tow bar. What is the total length of the car, tow bar and trailer? Show your working. Give your answer in metres.

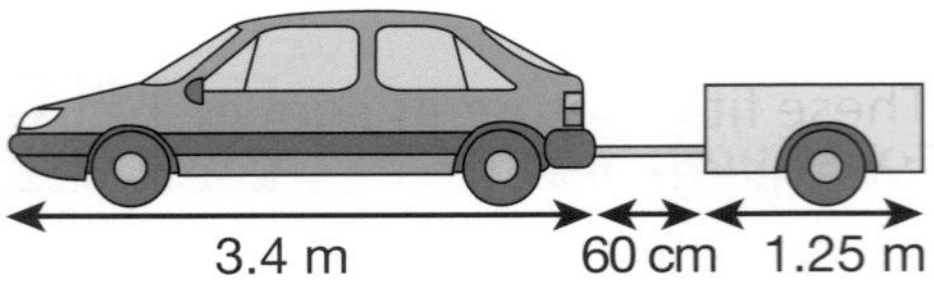

3.4 m   60 cm   1.25 m

_____ m

8. Liquid plant food is made by dissolving **15 grams** of plant food crystals in **4 litres** of water.
A gardener wants to make **20 litres** of liquid plant food.
How much plant food should he use? Show your working.

_____ grams

9. Patrick has some **20p**, **50p** and **£1** coins.
He can use the coins to make £2.60.
Complete the table to show the different ways he can make **£2.60**.

Number of 20p coins	Number of 50p coins	Number of £1 coins
13	0	0

10. You may use a calculator for this question.

Amy and Jade are planning to go on holiday together.
Amy uses the internet to find that the hotel room for the two of them costs **£39.80 per night**. They want to stay **7 nights**. The return flight costs **£234.75 each**.

Jade uses the travel agent to find out the package price of the holiday. The price is **£379 per person**. This includes the flights and the same shared room for 7 nights.

Which is the cheaper total price? _____
Show your working.

2 marks

11. Liam has made some tiles.
Here is one of his square tiles.

(a) On the grid, draw the tile after it
has been **rotated through 180°**.

1 mark

(b) Here is a different square tile.
Liam says that the design has
four lines of symmetry.
Explain why Liam is **wrong**.

1 mark

(c) Liam also has some rhombus-shaped
tiles. These fit together as shown.
Explain why the tiles fit together
without leaving any gaps.

70° 110°

1 mark

12. You may use a calculator for this question.
Calculate:

(a) 55% of £18.40. _____

1 mark

(b) $17\frac{1}{2}$ % of £74. _____

1 mark

13. Rajiv has a pack of cards. Each card
has either a letter or a number on it.
Each letter or number is either red
or black.
The table shows the number
of each type of card.

	Red	Black
Number	8	2
Letter	16	10

(a) How many cards are there in total? _____

1 mark

(b) What is the probability of picking a card with a black number? _____

1 mark

(c) All the cards with **red letters** are taken out of the pack.
Now what is the probability of picking a card with a black number? _____

1 mark

14. Write the correct sign (either <, > or =) to make each statement true.

(a) (−2) + 4 _____ 2

(b) 1 + (−4) _____ 3

(c) 3 − (−2) _____ 3 − 8

15. Part of this shape has been shaded.

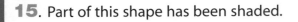

(a) What fraction of the shape has been shaded? _____

1 mark

(b) Write this fraction as a decimal. _____

1 mark

(c) Write the ratio of shaded parts to unshaded parts. _____

1 mark

16. Look at this calculation.

38.69 x 58.2

Carly says 'the answer to the multiplication must be **less than 2400**'.
Show how she knows this.
DO NOT work out the exact answer.

1 mark

17. The stem and leaf diagram shows the weights of 21 players in a football squad.

7 | 2   means 72 kg

(a) What is the weight of the heaviest player?

_____ kg

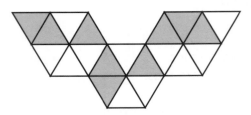

7	2 3 7 7
8	0 1 3 5 6 6 7 7 7 8 9
9	0 0 1 2 2 3

1 mark

(b) What is the modal weight? _____ kg

1 mark

(c) The table shows the number of goals scored by the squad in their last 20 matches. Work out the mean number of goals scored.

Number of goals scored	Number of matches
0	5
1	7
2	3
3	3
4	2

_____

2 marks

18. Complete each fraction to make each calculation correct.

(a) $\frac{4}{15} + \frac{\boxed{}}{15} = \frac{7}{15}$

(b) $\frac{2}{3} + \frac{\boxed{}}{15} = \frac{11}{15}$

(c) $\frac{\boxed{}}{3} + \frac{\boxed{}}{5} = \frac{8}{15}$

19. The pie chart shows how Mr Hall spends his **£800** monthly salary.
Mr Hall pays **£160 in tax** and **£320 on bills**.

Mr Hall

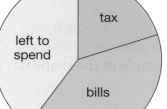

(a) What percentage of his salary is spent on **tax**?

_____ %

(b) What angle of the pie chart is needed to show **bills**?

_____ °

Mr Farmer

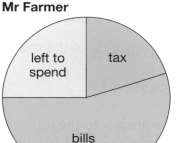

(c) This pie chart shows how Mr Farmer spends his salary of **£650**.
How much **tax** does Mr Farmer pay?
Tick one box.

more than Mr Hall ☐

less than Mr Hall ☐

the same as Mr Hall ☐   Explain your answer.

20. Tables and chairs are set out for meetings as shown.

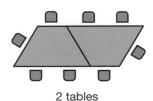
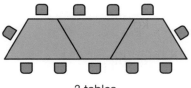

1 table
5 chairs

2 tables
8 chairs

3 tables
11 chairs

The rule that gives the number of chairs, **C**, needed for a given number of tables, **T**, is **C = 2 + 3T**.

(a) Use the rule to work out how many chairs are needed for **7 tables**.

_____

(b) Explain why it is not possible to seat exactly **33 people** at tables in this way with no empty spaces.

21. Work out the value of each expression given that:

$a = 5$ $b = 7$ $c = 8$

(a) $a + b - c =$ _____

1 mark

(b) $3c + 1 =$ _____

1 mark

(c) $b^2 - a^2 =$ _____

1 mark

22. Look at the rectangle and mirror line on the grid.

(a) **Reflect** the rectangle in the mirror line on the grid.

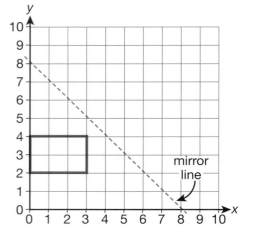

1 mark

(b) Circle the equation of the mirror line.

$y = 8x$ $y = x + 8$ $x + y = 8$ $x - 8 = y$ $y = 8$

1 mark

23. (a) Multiply $(3k + k + 8)$ by 2, simplifying your answer.

_____

2 marks

(b) The perimeter of the rectangular piece of paper is **40 cm**.
Work out the value of **k**.

_____

(k+8) cm

3k cm

2 marks

(c) This is a different rectangular piece of paper. It is folded in half then in half again along the dotted lines to make a smaller rectangle.
Write in the **length** and **width** of the smaller rectangle in terms of **m**.

2m + 6

4m

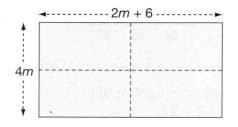

1 mark

Total

Possible total of 60 marks

GLOSSARY

adjacent	next to
area	the amount of space inside a 2D shape, measured in square units
biased	in probability, something which is not fair
bisect	cut in half
circumference	the perimeter of a circle
congruent	identical in size and shape
correlation	the connection between two quantities
denominator	the number on the bottom of a fraction
diagonal	a line drawn from one corner (**vertex**) to another that is not next to it
diameter	the distance from one side of a circle to the other passing through the centre
dimension	a length or distance on a shape
equation	in algebra, a statement in which the left hand side is equal to the right hand side
event	a situation where different things can happen based on chance
expression	in algebra, two or more **terms**
factor	a number which divides exactly into another
formula	in algebra, a rule written with letters to represent quantities
frequency	the number of times a number or outcome occurs
function	a set of mathematical instructions
integer	a positive or negative whole number
mean	the sum of all the values divided by the number of values
median	the middle value of a set of numbers when listed in order of size
mode	the item or number in a list that occurs most often
multiples	the answers to a multiplication table
net	how a 3D shape looks when folded out flat
numerator	the number on the top of a fraction
outcome	one possible thing that could happen in an **event**
parallel	lines which are the same distance apart
perimeter	the distance around a flat shape
perpendicular	lines which meet or intersect at right angles
polygon	a 2D shape with straight sides
power	the number of times a number is multiplied by itself
prime number	a number that can only be divided by one and itself
prism	a solid shape which has the same cross-section all the way through
product	the result when two numbers are multiplied
quadrilateral	a 2D shape with four sides
radius	the distance from the centre of a circle to the **circumference**
range	the difference between the largest and smallest numbers in a list
regular	a shape with all sides the same size and all angles the same size
root	the inverse operation of raising a number to a **power**
sample	a selection of people/items featured in a survey/experiment
scale factor	the number by which the **dimensions** of a shape are multiplied when enlarged
similar	the same shape but a different size
square number	a whole number multiplied by itself (that is, squared)
term	in algebra, a letter or combination of letters and a number
tessellation	a pattern where the shapes fit together without leaving gaps
vertex	a corner of a 2D or 3D shape (vertices is plural of vertex)
volume	the amount of space filled by a 3D object

ANSWERS TO ACTIVITIES FOR WEEKS 1-8

Week 1 Monday

1 D B C A
2 No. The number 4.9 has 9 tenths whilst the number 4.86 has only 8 tenths so 4.9 is bigger. The > sign is the wrong way round. *You can only get the mark if your answer includes the correct explanation. Just ticking No is not enough.*
3(a) 0.723   **(b)** 37.2   **(c)** 7.32 and 0.723
4(a) 430 (= 4.3 x 100)   **(b)** 0.43 (= 43 ÷ 100)
5(a) 5961   **(b)** 5619
6(a) 1000   **(b)** 0.22   **(c)** 10   **(d)** 40
7 100 x 23 = 2300p = £23.00, 1000 x 45 = 45000p = £450.00, 10 x £6.49 = £64.90. *Award 2 marks if you worked out these three multiplications correctly. Award 1 mark for two out of three correct.*
£23.00 + £450.00 + £64.90 = £537.90. *Award the final mark if you calculated this total correctly. If you just show the correct final answer you will get all 3 marks but it is best to show all your working out as you can still get some marks even if your final answer is incorrect.*

Week 1 Tuesday

1(a) Tuesday (the difference between 6 and –5 is 11)
(b) 3°C (since –8 + 11 = 3)
2 10 – 15; –10 + 5; 5 x (–1). *Award 2 marks for all three correct. If you got two correct and did not circle more than three calculations, award 1 mark.*
3(a) 2 (4 x 3 = 12 points and 5 x –2 = –10 points giving 12 – 10 = 2)
(b) –3 (3 x 3 = 9 points and 6 x –2 = –12 points giving 9 – 12 = –3)
4(a) –7 < 7   **(b)** –6 < –4
5(a) Forward 6 squares since –3 x –2 = 6
(b) Back 3 squares since 3 x –1 = –3   **(c)** 1 and 2 or –2 and –1
6(a) –7, –1   **(b)** 6, –3   **(c)** –3, 1

Week 1 Wednesday

1(a) $5n$ **(b)** $2(n + 5)$ or $(n + 5)$ x 2 or $2n + 10$ but **not** 2 x n + 5
2(a) $k – j$ **(b)** $k + 3$ **(c)** $2j$ or 2 x j
3(a) $2m + 4$ **(b)** $6h$ **(c)** $6b + 17$ **(d)** $5a + 4m$ **(e)** $7st$ **(f)** $9p + 4p^2$
4(a) $3n + 3$ or $3(n + 1)$ (simplify $n + 3 + 2n$)   **(b)** $n + 1$
5(a) $2a$ **(b)** $8m$ **(c)** $15a + 5$ **(d)** $n^2 + 2n$ **(e)** $3m + 6 + 2m + 2 = 5m + 8$

Week 1 Thursday

1(a) 800 (x 100)   **(b)** 9 (÷ 1000)   **(c)** 23000 (x 1000)   **(d)** 5 (ml are same as cm³)   **(e)** 3.5 (÷ 100)   **(f)** 4500 (x 1000)   **(g)** 520 (x 100)
(h) 700 (x 1000)   **(i)** 0.45 (÷ 1000)   **(j)** 5.8 (÷ 1000)
2 300 g. *Convert 0.03 kg to 30 g and 3000 mg to 3 g so that all the masses are in the same units, grams. You can now see that 300 g is the heaviest.*
3 1.9 km. *Convert 700 m to 0.7 km then add to 1.2 km.*
4 16. *Convert 4 kg to 4000 g and divide by 25 or work out that you can get four 250 g bags from 1 kg so you can get 4 x 4 (= 16) bags from 4 kg.*
5 0.65 litres. *Convert 850 ml into 0.85 litres then subtract from 1.5 litres.*
6(a) An answer between 150 and 180 grams   **(b)** 24 km
(c) 6 or 6.6 pounds   **(d)** 4 gallons

Week 1 Friday

1 Right-angled and isosceles. *Both types are needed to get the mark.*
2 Possible pentagons include

3 No. A rhombus has four equal sides but in this shape the diagonal sides are longer than the horizontal sides. *You must have both parts correct for the mark. Your explanation must mention that the shape does not have four equal sides.*
4 Kite and rhombus. *Draw in the sides of the shapes to help you see what the shapes actually look like.*
5(a) The sum of the angles in a triangle is 180°. A quadrilateral is made up of 2 triangles so the angles must add up to 2 x 180° = 360°.   **(b)** 720°. *Since a hexagon divides into 4 triangles, the angles must add up to 4 x 180° = 720°.*   **(c)** 8 sides. *Divide 1080° by 180° to find out that this polygon is made up of 6 triangles, so the shape has 8 sides.*
6 a = 50° (180° – 48° – 82°) b = 195° (360° – 70° – 65° – 30°)

Week 2 Monday

1(a) 175   **(b)** 1242   **(c)** 123   **(d)** 5465
2(a) 26.42   **(b)** 25.62   **(c)** 28.68   **(d)** 4.03
3(a) 0.12   **(b)** 0.035   **(c)** 0.0045
4(a) 4   **(b)** 7
5 1118. *Award both marks if the final answer is correct. Award 1 mark if you have some correct working, for example, 43 x 6=258 and 43 x 20 = 860, but then an incorrect final answer.*
6 16. *Award both marks if your final answer is correct. In the Test you would score 1 mark if you have some correct working.*

Week 2 Tuesday

1(a) 8   **(b)** 25   **(c)** 49   **(d)** 81   **(e)** 100 000   **(f)** 27
2(a) 9   **(b)** 8   **(c)** 2   **(d)** 10   **(e)** 12   **(f)** 5
3(a) 2^5. *Work out the value of each index number to compare them:* 2^5 = 32, 4^2 = 16, 3^3 = 27, 9^1 = 9, 1^{10} = 1.   **(b)** 9^1
4(a) 4 (=14 – 10)   **(b)** 13 (= 23 – 10)   **(c)** 12 (= 3 x 4)   **(d)** 25 (= 5 + 24 – 4)   **(e)** 12 (= 4 + 8)   **(f)** 10 (= 2^2 + 6 = 4 + 6)
5(a) (6 + 3) x 5 – 2   **(b)** (6 + 3) x (5 – 2)

Week 2 Wednesday

1 17 and 5. *Only these two numbers must be circled to gain the mark.*
2 2 x 3 x 3 x 7 or in index form 2 x 3^2 x 7. *Award 1 mark if you have found three out of the four correct prime factors and both marks if you have all four correct.*
3(a) 1, 2, 7, 14   **(b)** 28   **(c)** 5 years. *Andrea will be 19 (14 + 5) and Ben will be 29 (24 + 5).*
4(a) 16 = 1 x 16, 16 = 2 x 8, 16 = 4 x 4 so factors are 1, 2, 4, 8 and 16. *All three factor pairs must be correct to gain the mark.*   **(b)** One of the factor pairs of a square number is the same number multiplied by itself so this only counts as one factor. Every other factor pair gives two different factors. This means the number of factors for a square number will always be odd. *Award the mark if your explanation is similar to this one.*
5(a) Cross out 27 (it is not a square number).   **(b)** Possible numbers are 4, 64, 144 (there are more). *Your number must also be written in the intersection (middle part) of the diagram to get the mark.*
6 3 rows of 16, 4 rows of 12, 6 rows of 8, 8 rows of 6. *Award 1 mark if you have three out of the four possible combinations, and 2 marks if you have exactly these four correct. To work out the answer to this question it is a good idea to start by listing all the factor pairs for 48 and working out which ones are not allowed.*

Week 2 Thursday

1(a) Perimeter 12 cm, area 5 cm². *Both answers are needed to gain the mark.*
(b) Possible shapes include

Your shape should not have any diagonal lines and should not be a rectangle.

2 C. *C has an area of $4\frac{1}{2}$ cm² whilst the other four shapes have an area of 4 cm².*
3

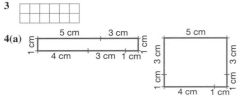

4(a)

(b) No. The total length of the rods is 18 m. To make a square with this perimeter would require sides of length 4.5 m (18 ÷ 4). There are no 0.5 m lengths of rod so it could not be made. *You need to tick No and give an explanation along the line of the one above to gain the mark.*
5(a)   **(b)** 18 cm (= 5 + 4 + 3 + 5 + 1 cm)

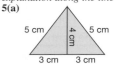

Week 2 Friday

1(a) 5 white and 5 black   **(b)** 10 black   **(c)** 6 white and 4 black, or 7 white and 3 black, or 8 white and 2 black, or 9 white and 1 black. *These combinations ensure that there are more white than black so the chances of picking white are greater than for black.*
2(a) 2   **(b)** $\frac{1}{8}$

(c) 0.25 (= $\frac{2}{8}$ = $\frac{1}{4}$). *You must give your answer as a decimal. Do not award the mark if you have written a fraction.*
3 AA, AP, AO, AB, PP, PO, PB, OO, OB, BB. *You must have all ten combinations and no extras to gain the mark. Be careful here that you do not repeat some answers, for example, AP and PA are the same combination of fruit and only count once.*
4 Numbers must include one 5, one odd number other than 5, and four even numbers which may or may not be different. *Award 1 mark if you have done two of these three things on your spinner.*
5 Although there are three different types of sweets the chance of picking each is not necessarily equally likely. There may be different numbers of each type of sweet making it more likely that one sweet could be picked than another. *Award the mark if your explanation points out that there may not be the same number of each sweet in the bag.*

Week 3 Monday

1 £5.68 (total of items is £4.32). *Award 1 mark if you have correctly calculated the total for the items but worked out the change incorrectly. You may also award a mark if you have worked out the change correctly for an incorrect total. Check this on a calculator.*
2 1.15 kg (total sold is 1.35 kg). *Award 1 mark if you worked out 1.35 kg is the amount sold. Both marks for a correct final answer.*
3 27 (division gives 26 remainder 12). *Award 1 mark for some correct working or if you gave the answer 26 coaches. Notice that the answer to the division is rounded up to 27. You must give 27 as your final answer to gain both marks.*
4 Mr Reid £50.00, Miss Quinn £53.00. *Award 1 mark for each part. Miss Quinn's order includes a £5.00 delivery charge as the total cost of her items is only £48.00.*
5(a) 864 packets. *Award 1 mark for some correct working and both marks if the final answer is correct.* **(b)** £43.20

Week 3 Tuesday

1(a) 75 minutes (= 2 x 25 + 25) **(b)** 85 minutes (= 3 x 20 + 15)
2(a) £1.25 (4 x 15 + 65 = 125, then ÷ 100) **(b)** 10 miles (inverse operations in reverse order: 2.15 x 100 = 215, then – 65 gives 150, then ÷ 15)
3(a) 14 **(b)** –2
4 40
5 10
6 30, 14, 3

Week 3 Wednesday

1(a) 26 cm² **(b)** 81 mm² **(c)** 10 cm² **(d)** 6 km² **(e)** 40 cm² **(f)** 48 cm²
(g) 5 m²
2(a) 8 cm. *Ask 'What length must be multiplied by itself to get 64?'*
(b) 4 cm. *Divide the area by 16 to get the length of the other side.*
3(a)

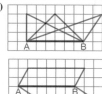

Your triangle must have a height of 3 cm – various triangles are possible.

(b)

Your parallelogram must have a height of 2 cm – various parallelograms are possible.

Week 3 Thursday

1(a) 475 grams **(b)** 1.6 litres **(c)** 3.75 kg
2(a) 114° **(b)** 38°
3 and 4 *Ask someone to check your constructions, checking that angles and lines are accurate. Make sure you leave in your construction lines even if they make them look a bit untidy. The person marking your Test looks for evidence of your constructions. Also, be as accurate as you can. You will lose marks if your angles and lines are not accurately drawn.*

Week 3 Friday

1(a) Add one tally mark to the first row, add one to the second row, add two to the third row and one to the fifth row. The frequencies should be 8, 11, 6, 3, 2. *You must have all five frequencies correct to gain the mark.*
(b) 19
2 Kim. Kim's method allows her to organise her results as she collects them. She can see at a glance the most common number of people in a car. Tyrone will have to sort out his data after he has collected it. *You must tick Kim and give a similar explanation to gain the mark.*
3(a) Some of the ranges overlap. It is not clear, for example, which box you would tick if you are 25. There are two possible boxes you could tick. **(b)** There are not enough answers to choose from. There are more than two eye colours. **(c)** It is not clear what is meant by these words. For example, sometimes could mean once a week or three times a week.
4 Sanjay has not asked enough people. He will not have asked a good cross-section of people. Many are at work or school at this time. *Your reasons must be different. One should be about the number of people asked and the other should be about the time of day he carried out the survey.*

Week 4 Monday

1(a) 46000 **(b)** 90 **(c)** 40 **(d)** 4000 **(e)** 70000 **(f)** 400 **(g)** 1
(h) 1000
2(a) 19.8 **(b)** 13.3 **(c)** 6.05 **(d)** 16.21 **(e)** 4.1 **(f)** 0.03
3 27 m². *Award 1 mark for working out the area as 4.35 x 6.27 = 27.2745 m². Award the second mark if you have rounded correctly. You may also award a mark if you calculated the area incorrectly but rounded this answer correctly.*
4 18p. *Award 1 mark for working out the price of a pear as 1.25 ÷ 7 = 0.17857... Award the second mark if you have rounded correctly to £0.18 or 18p. You may also award a mark if you calculated the price of a pear incorrectly but rounded this answer correctly.*
5 107. *Award 1 mark if you rounded each number to give (900 ÷ 9) + (7 x 1). Award the second mark if you correctly worked this out to give 107. You do not get any marks if you worked out the calculation exactly as this question is trying to test your estimation skills.*

6 800 cm². *Award 1 mark if you rounded each number to give 20 x 40. Award the second mark if you correctly worked this out to give 800 cm². You do not get any marks if you worked out the calculation exactly as this question is trying to test your estimation skills.*

Week 4 Tuesday

1(a) 1681 **(b)** 1.96 **(c)** 324 **(d)** 28.3024 **(e)** 3.375 **(f)** 65.1249
(g) 1331 **(h)** 0.000064
2(a) 8.6 **(b)** 2.1 **(c)** 4.2 **(d)** 5.5 **(e)** 2.9 **(f)** 1.2
3(a) 25.07 **(b)** 0.48 **(c)** 15.87 **(d)** 1.76 **(e)** 0.19 **(f)** 1.42

Week 4 Wednesday

1 46, 42, 38, 34, 30. *All five terms must be correct to gain the mark.*
2(a) 6, 48 **(b)** –2, –8. *In each part both terms must be correct to gain the mark.*
3 3, 9. *Both terms must be correct to gain the mark.*
4(a) 5h + 1 **(b)** 76. *You can gain the mark for part (b) if you have chosen the incorrect formula in part (a) but have correctly substituted h = 15 into it.*
5(a) 5n + 2 **(b)** 5n – 6
6 4n – 3 (or n x 4 – 3, or 4 x n – 3). *Award 1 mark if your formula has 4n in it but not – 3. Award both marks only for the correct formula.*

Week 4 Thursday

1(a) 28.27 cm **(b)** 75.40 cm
2(a) 452.4 cm² **(b)** 7854.0 cm²
3 28.6 cm. *Work out 90 ÷ π.*
4 6.9 m. *Work out square root of 150 ÷ π.*
5 14137 cm (or 141.37 m). *Award 1 mark if you worked out the circumference as 45 x π = 141.37... then award the second mark if you then multiplied this by 100 to get 14137 cm (nearest cm).*
6(a) 6.28 m². *Award 1 mark if you worked out the area of a circle of radius 2 m and got 12.566... m². Award the second mark if you then halved your answer since the lawn is half a circle.* **(b)** 10.28 m. *Award 1 mark if you worked out the circumference of a circle of radius 2 m (that is diameter 4 m) and got 12.566... m. Award the second mark if you then halved your answer and added 4 m (the straight edge of the lawn).*

Week 4 Friday

1 38
2 169 cm. *Median is the number half way between 168 cm and 170 cm.*
3 Mean 41.94 kg, range 6.8 kg
4(a) Alan has a higher mean which suggests that he generally did better in the tests than Ellie. **(b)** Alan's range is much larger than Ellie's which suggests that Alan scored some high and some low marks. Ellie's marks were more similar.
5(a) Mean is 8.1 (to 1 decimal place), range is 1.5. *1 mark each for the mean and range.* **(b)** Mean is 8, range is 0.5. *1 mark each for the mean and range.* **(c)** Judges can give biased marks. By missing off the highest and lowest the extreme values are lost and only the more representative scores are used.
6 3, 5 and 6. *The mode is 6 which means that at least 2 cards must have the number 6. Since the mean is 5 the total of the four cards must be 4 x 5 = 20. If two of the cards are 6 the other two must have a total of 8. To give a range of 3 these numbers must be 3 and 5. Award 1 mark if you worked out that one of the cards is 6 and you have shown somewhere in your working that the total is 20. You can only get both marks if you stated all three numbers correctly.*

Week 5 Monday

1(a) $\frac{3}{5}$ **(b)** $\frac{1}{3}$

2(a) 9 **(b)** 48 **(c)** 2
3(a) Shade any 2 out of the 16 parts. **(b)** Shade any 12 out of the 20 parts. **(c)** Shade any 6 out of the 24 parts.
4(a) $1\frac{3}{5}$ **(b)** $1\frac{5}{7}$ **(c)** $4\frac{3}{4}$

5(a) $\frac{11}{3}$ **(b)** $\frac{11}{5}$ **(c)** $\frac{49}{10}$

6

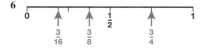

Week 5 Tuesday

1(a) 0.4 **(b)** 0.71 **(c)** 0.15 **(d)** 0.375
2(a) $\frac{1}{20}$ (= $\frac{5}{100}$) **(b)** $\frac{9}{50}$ (= $\frac{18}{100}$) **(c)** $1\frac{1}{5}$ = $\frac{6}{5}$ (= $\frac{120}{100}$).

Each fraction must be in its simplest terms to gain each mark.
3(a) 39% = $\frac{39}{100}$ **(b)** 4% = $\frac{1}{25}$

4 $\frac{5}{32}$ is greater. *Divide the numerator by the denominator to get each fraction as a decimal.* $\frac{5}{32}$ = 0.15625 *and* $\frac{3}{20}$ = 0.15. *You must show your working to gain the mark.*

5(a) Shade in any 3 parts of the diagram. **(b)** Shade in any 5 parts of the diagram.
6(a) $\frac{1}{5}$ **(b)** $\frac{73}{100}$. *Your answers must be fractions. No marks for giving the answers as decimals.*

Week 5 Wednesday

1(a) 9, −2, 3 **(b)** 13, 7, −3. *For each part award 2 marks for all three values correct. Award 1 mark for each part for two out of three correct.*
2(a) ÷ 5 **(b)** + 1 and x 3 in this order
3(a) 6, 4, 2, 0
(b)

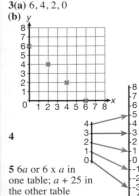

Award 1 mark for correctly working out all four values. If you have one or more incorrect values you do not get the mark. Award 1 mark for correctly plotting all four points. You still gain this mark if your values to the first part were incorrect but you have correctly plotted them. If one point is incorrectly plotted you lose the mark.

4

5 6*a* or 6 x *a* in one table; *a* + 25 in the other table

Week 5 Thursday

1(a) 6 faces, 12 edges, 8 vertices **(b)** 5 faces, 8 edges, 5 vertices. *All three values must be correct to gain the mark for each part.*
2 Shape (b) does not have the same cross-section all the way through it so it is not a prism.
3

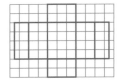

4(a) 5 **(b)** 4
5(a)

(b) Possible answers include

The colours of the cubes are not important for this answer.
6

Others are possible.

Week 5 Friday

1(a) 55 **(b)** No. Some boys may study more than one language. 80 represents the total number of choices rather than the total number of boys. *You must tick No and give a suitable explanation to gain the mark. This explanation is quite difficult to put into words. If you find it difficult try giving an example to illustrate your thinking. For example, 80 could represent 40 boys each choosing 2 languages.*
2(a) An answer in the range £26 to £28
(b)

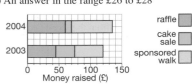

3(a) 38 minutes **(b)** 25 minutes **(c)** 21 minutes
4(a) Between June and December **(b)** No. Sales in August are 6000. If they had doubled the December sales would be 12000 but they are only 8000. *You must tick No and give a suitable explanation to gain the mark. This question is testing whether you have read the scale on the graph properly – it just looks like sales have doubled in the graph because the scale does not start at zero.*

Week 6 Monday

Answers to questions 1 to 4 must be fractions in their lowest terms to gain each mark.
1(a) $\frac{5}{11}$ **(b)** $\frac{3}{4}$ (= $\frac{6}{8}$) **(c)** $1\frac{2}{7}$ (= $\frac{9}{7}$) **(d)** $1\frac{2}{5}$ (= $\frac{21}{15}$ = $\frac{7}{5}$)
2(a) $\frac{5}{12}$ **(b)** $1\frac{16}{21}$ **(c)** $\frac{1}{8}$ **(d)** $1\frac{4}{15}$
3(a) $\frac{14}{27}$ **(b)** $\frac{15}{28}$ **(c)** $\frac{1}{2}$
4(a) $\frac{15}{16}$ **(b)** $\frac{7}{8}$ **(c)** $1\frac{1}{5}$
5 $\frac{1}{3}$. *Award 1 mark if you added together $\frac{2}{5}$ and $\frac{1}{15}$ to give $\frac{10}{15}$, or $\frac{2}{3}$. Since $\frac{2}{3}$ go home or have packed lunch then $\frac{1}{3}$ must have a school lunch.*

Week 6 Tuesday

1(a)

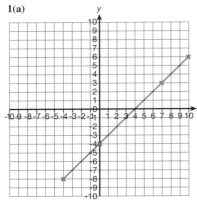

(b) No. If you substitute the *x*- and *y*-coordinates of this point into the equation for the line you get 27 = 30 − 4 which does not balance. This shows that the point does not lie on the line. *You must tick No and give a suitable explanation for the mark. Your explanation must show that the values x = 30 and y = 27 don't work in the equation.*
2 5, 7, 11, 13. *Gain both marks if you have all four y-values correct. Award 1 mark if you have any three out of four correct.*
3 E, C, A, B, D. *Award 3 marks only if all five are correct. Score 2 marks for three out of five correct and 1 mark if two are correct.*
4 $y = \frac{1}{2}x + 3$ and $y = \frac{1}{2}x$. *Only these two must be indicated to gain the mark.*
5 $x + y = 7$
6(a) An answer in the range 56 to 58 euros **(b)** £280. The graph does not extend this far but you can use the graph to read off that £70 is 100 euros. Multiplying by four gives £280 for 400 euros. *Your answer must show your reasoning in words and/or numbers.*

Week 6 Wednesday

1(a) 240 **(b)** 6 **(c)** 150 **(d)** 105 **(e)** 2 hours 15 minutes
2 1.5 hours, 1 hour 40 minutes, 105 minutes. *Change each time to minutes and compare them: 1.5 hours = 90 minutes, 1 hour 40 minutes = 100 minutes.*
3 3 hours 36 minutes. *Award 1 mark if you added the minutes together to give 96 minutes, or if you changed 2 hours 45 minutes to 165 minutes. Award both marks if your answer is correct and given in minutes and hours, not just in minutes.*
4(a) 2 hours 16 minutes **(b)** 25 minutes
5 13 minutes 45 seconds (or $13\frac{3}{4}$ minutes). *Award 1 mark for calculating that the 5 laps she runs take 8 minutes 45 seconds, both marks for a correct final answer. You cannot have a mark if the only part you calculated correctly is that she jogs for 5 minutes – too easy!*

Week 6 Thursday

1(a) 105 cm³ **(b)** 6000 cm³
2(a) 18 cm³ **(b)** Two of these three combinations – 1 cm x 1 cm x 18 cm, 1 cm x 2 cm x 9 cm, 1 cm x 3 cm x 6 cm. *You must have two different cuboids. For example, note that 1 x 3 x 6 is the same cuboid as 3 x 1 x 6.*
3 30. *Award 1 mark if you correctly calculated both the volume of the box (240 cm³) and the volume of a cube (8 cm³) but did not get the final answer correct.*
4(a) 64 cm² **(b)** 32 cm³
5(a) 24 000 cm³ **(b)** 24 litres
6 10 cm. *Award 1 mark if you attempted to substitute the values into the volume formula but got an incorrect final answer. For example, 180 = x x 3 x 6.*

Week 6 Friday

1(a) *Check that all your points are plotted accurately. Deduct 1 mark if you have one or two incorrect points. More than two points incorrectly plotted scores nothing.*

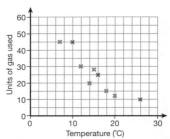

(b) Negative. The hotter the weather the less gas is likely to be used for heating and cooking. *You must give the reason for the correlation shown.*
2(a) The taller the person, the larger their feet.
(b) (c) (d)

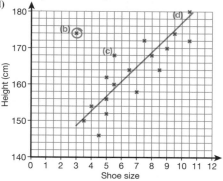

(e) Your answer should be in the range 158–162 cm.   **(f)** None of the data points includes people with a size as small as 2. It cannot be assumed that the relationship is the same for smaller shoe sizes.
3 Negative, none, positive. *Award 1 mark if any two are correct, both marks if all three are correct.*

Week 7 Monday

1 9B is $\frac{2}{3}$, 9C is $\frac{4}{9}$, 9H is $\frac{8}{15}$

2 Maths 90%, English 80%, Science 75%
3(a) 39 kg   **(b)** £6.30
4(a) £13.50   **(b)** 106.6 km
5 35.6% (rounded to 1 decimal place) or 36% (rounded to nearest whole number). *Award 1 mark if your final answer is incorrect but you have correctly calculated that she has £9130 of her salary left and you have attempted to work out this amount as a percentage of £25650. That is*

$\frac{9130}{25650}$ *x 100.*

6 £7871 (to nearest £). *Award 1 mark if you correctly worked out that $12\frac{1}{2}$ % of 8995 is 1124.375. To get your final answer remember to subtract this amount from 8995. Round your answer to the nearest £.*

Week 7 Tuesday

1(a) 4 : 3   **(b)** 3 : 2   **(c)** 2 : 3 : 7
2(a) 5 : 19   **(b)** 1 : 3.8
3 18 m²
4 100 ml
5(a) 45 grams   **(b)** 60 grams
6(a) The path is 18 squares and the lawn is 10 squares. The ratio of lawn to path is 10 : 18 = 5 : 9.   **(b)** $\frac{5}{14}$

Week 7 Wednesday

1(a) $y = 3$ **(b)** $k = 6$ **(c)** $m = 6$ **(d)** $t = \frac{3}{4}$ **(e)** $q = -1$

2(a) $a = 3$. *Award 1 mark if you found that $5a = 15$ but got an incorrect value for a.*   **(b)** $q = 5$. *Award 1 mark if you found that $4q = 20$ but got an incorrect value for q.*   **(c)** $t = \frac{1}{2}$. *Award 1 mark if you found that $6t = 3$ but got an incorrect value for t.*
3(a) $3a + 4a + a + 7 = 47$ which simplifies to $8a + 7 = 47$ **(b)** $a = 5$ cm
4 x lies between 5.6 and 5.7. *Award 1 mark if you correctly completed the values for 6 and 5.5 in the table as 42, too big and 35.75, too small. Score a second mark if you then correctly found values for 5.6 and 5.7.*

Week 7 Thursday

1(a) 113°   **(b)** 30°   **(c)** 83°
2(a) (b)

(a) angles marked ■ are same size
angles marked □ are same size
(b) any pair with one marked ■ and one marked □ add up to 180°

3 $a = 130°, b = 50°, c = 50°, d = 50°$. *You need to get all four correct for 3 marks. Score 2 marks for three correct angles and 1 mark for two correct angles.*
4 80°
5 $a = 42°, b = 132°, c = 38°$. *Award 1 mark for each correct angle.*
6 $a = 70°$

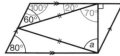

Score 3 marks for the correct answer. Award 1 mark if you found any of the angles, other than a, marked on the diagram. Award 2 marks for any two of the angles, other than a, marked on the diagram.

Week 7 Friday

1(a) $\frac{1}{8}$ **(b)** 45 grams

2(a) 80°   **(b)** 18, 24, 16, 6. *Award 1 mark for three out of four correct and 2 marks for all four correct.*
3 20, 30, 15, 35. *Award 1 mark for two correct, 2 marks for three correct and 3 marks for all four correct.*
4 Angles are 96°, 212°, 52°

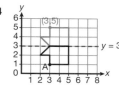

more than 4 hours — less than 2 hours — 2-4 hours

Score 1 mark for correctly working out all three angles. Score 2 marks for an accurately drawn pie chart and 1 mark if your angles are not very accurate (+ or – 2° out). Ask someone to check this for you.

5(a) Saturday   **(b)** Can't tell

Week 8 Monday

1(a) No lines of symmetry, order 2   **(b)** 4 lines of symmetry, order 4
2

3

4

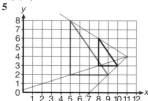

Coordinates of A are (3, 5). *1 mark for the reflection, 1 for the coordinates.*

5 90, anticlockwise, (3, 2). *All three must be correct to gain the mark.*

Week 8 Tuesday

1(a) A and E   **(b)** F and A (or E)
2 5 squares to the right, 3 squares down
3 16 cm, 20 cm, 35°. *Award 2 marks for all three correct. Score 1 mark for any two correct.*
4 (3, 2)
5

Award 1 mark if you correctly enlarged the shape but did not draw it in the correct position. For both marks you must have drawn your shape the correct size and in the correct position as shown.

Week 8 Wednesday

1(a) 676. *Your working should show that you have added the answers for 10 x 52 and 3 x 52 together (or some other suitable combination, for example 6 x 52 and 7 x 52).*   **(b)** 9. *Your working should show that you have used the fact 9 x 52 = 468.*   **(c)** 312. *Your working should show that you have used the fact 6 x 52, for 1 mark, and then shown that 6 x 52 can be written as 12 x 26 for the second mark.*
2(a) 0.9375. *This can be worked out by realising that $\frac{31}{16} = 1\frac{15}{16}$.*
(b) $\frac{39}{40}$. *This can be worked out by realising that $3 \times \frac{13}{40}$ is $\frac{39}{40}$.*
3(a) £6. *Since 10% is £4 and 5% is £2.*   **(b)** £1.60. *Since 10% is 50p, then 30% is £1.50 and 2% is 10p.*   **(c)** £45. *Since £2 is 5% of £40 and 25p is 5% of £5.*   **(d)** 6%. *Since £2 is 5% of £40 and 40p is 1% of £40.*
4 680. *For 1 mark you should show that the number is 20 x 34, for the second mark you must work out the multiplication: 2 x 34 = 68 then x 10 to give 680.*
5(a) 5. *This is found by dividing each term in the first equation by 2.*
(b) Replace $2k$ in the first equation by $j + a$ from the second equation to give $4j + j + a = 10$ which simplifies to $5j + a = 10$.

Week 8 Thursday

1(a)

(b)

2(a)
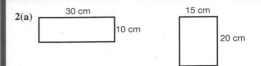

(b) 80 cm (for the 30 x 10 rectangle) and 70 cm (for the 20 x 15 rectangle)
3(a) 120° **(b)** Three hexagons fit together exactly. The three angles that fit together are each 120° which gives a total of 360°.
4

Week 8 Friday

1(a) 25 **(b)** $\frac{1}{5}$. *Out of a total of 150 fish, 30 were small cod.* $\frac{30}{150}$ *simplifies to* $\frac{1}{5}$. **(c)** 2. *In the table 21 out of 150 chose small haddock, so you could expect about 2 out of 15 to choose the same.*
2 *The people Oliver asked would probably have found it easier to park at that time than those Robert asked. The responses they gave are likely to be based on that day's experiences.*
3(a) 110 g. *Although 4 g is the most popular answer it is incorrect – these pupils have read the ounces scale. Since 110 g is the next most popular answer this is the most likely mass. Both parts must be correct to gain the mark.* **(b)** 4.5 kg. *Award 1 mark for showing that the total mass is 50 x 90 g = 4500 g. Award a second mark for converting to 4.5 kg.*
4(a) $\frac{3}{16}$ **(b)**

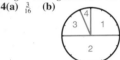

ANSWERS TO PRACTICE TEST

1(a) 728 **(b)** 9
2(a) Square-based pyramid **(b)** 48 cm²
3(a) 4762 **(b)** Either 72 + 64 or 74 + 62
4(a)

Award 1 mark if you have drawn the shape the correct way round but have not used the dotted paper correctly.

(b) 16 cm²
5(a) 4, 0.4 **(b)** 5, 320. *For each part you must have both missing numbers correct to gain the mark.*
6(a) 180° **(b)** 72°
7 5.25 m. *Award both marks for a correct answer. If your answer was incorrect but you correctly wrote down that 60 cm = 0.6 m, award 1 mark.*
8 75 grams. *Award 1 mark if you got the wrong answer but wrote down that you need to multiply the amount of crystals (15 grams) by 5.*
9

Number of 20p coins	Number of 50p coins	Number of £1 coins
13	0	0
3	0	2
3	4	0
3	2	1
8	0	1
8	2	0

Award 3 marks if you got all five other combinations correct. Award 2 marks for any four different correct combinations and 1 mark for any three different correct combinations.
10 Amy's price is cheaper.
Amy's price: £39.80 x 7 + £234.75 x 2 = £748.10
Jade's price: £379 x 2 = £758
You must show your working to gain the marks. Simply stating that Amy's price is cheaper will gain no marks if you do not show some relevant calculations. Award 1 mark for each correct total price.
11(a)

(b) Although the square tile has a square border, giving it 4 lines of symmetry, the design in the centre only has 2 lines. The overall design has just 2 lines of symmetry. **(c)** The angles where four tiles fit together add up to exactly 360° so there are no gaps.
12(a) £10.12 **(b)** £12.95

13(a) 36 **(b)** $\frac{2}{36}$ or $\frac{1}{18}$. *You cannot gain the mark if you have written the probability as 2 out of 36 or 1 out of 18.* **(c)** $\frac{2}{20}$ or $\frac{1}{10}$
14(a) = **(b)** < (*since* –3 < 3) **(c)** > (*since* 5 > –5)
15(a) $\frac{9}{20}$ **(b)** 0.45 **(c)** 9 : 11
16 Carly could round up both numbers to 40 and 60 and multiply to give 2400. Since both numbers are smaller than the rounded values, the answer must be smaller than 2400. *You do not get a mark if you have attempted to work out the exact calculation.*
17(a) 93 kg **(b)** 87 kg **(c)** 1.5. *Award 1 mark if you correctly calculated the total number of goals as 30. Award a mark if you got the total number of goals wrong but attempted to divide your (incorrect) total by 20.*
18(a) 3 **(b)** 1 **(c)** 1, 1
19(a) 20% **(b)** 144° **(c)** Tick 'less than Mr Hall' and give the correct explanation – the tax sectors on both pie charts are the same size but since Mr Farmer earns less than Mr Hall his tax must be less than Mr Hall's. *You must tick the correct box and give the correct explanation to gain the mark.*
20(a) 23 chairs **(b)** 10 tables would seat exactly 32 people. 11 tables would be needed to seat 33 people but there would be some empty spaces around this table.
21(a) 4 **(b)** 25 **(c)** 24
22(a) **(b)** $x + y = 8$

23(a) $8k + 16$. *Award 2 marks for the correct answer. Award 1 mark for some correct working – either showing that the bracket simplifies to 4k + 8 or that each term in the bracket multiplies by 2 to give 6k + 2k + 16.* **(b)** 3. *Award 1 mark if you have got the wrong answer but have written down an equation such as 8k + 16 = 40, or 2(3k + k + 8) = 40.* **(c)** m + 3 (longer side); 2m (shorter side). *Both must be correct to gain the mark.*

Awarding a level for the practice test

Work out your total score out of a possible total of 60 marks. Use the table to work out the level you have achieved in **this test**. This is only a guide to the level at which you are working but should give you an idea of how you could expect to perform in the Tests.

Level	Marks
N	0–8
3	9–11
4	12–21
5	22–33
6	34–60